Lernkrimi Englisch

Long Time No Kill

W0195362

Caroline Simpson

compact

Weitere Informationen zu Compact Lernkrimis finden Sie am Ende des Buches und unter www.lernkrimi.de.

© Compact Verlag GmbH
Baierbrunner Straße 27, 81379 München
Ausgabe 2015

Chefredaktion: Dr. Matthias Feldbaum
Redaktion: Helga Aichele
Fachkorrektur: Nathalie Russell
Produktion: Ute Hausleiter
Titelillustration: Karl Knospe
Lernkrimi-Logo: Carsten Abelbeck
Gestaltung: EKH Werbeagentur GbR, textum GmbH
Umschlaggestaltung: EKH Werbeagentur GbR, Hartmut Baier

ISBN 978-3-8174-9794-2
381749794/1

www.compactverlag.de, www.lernkrimi.de, www.facebook.com/lernkrimi

Vorwort

Liebe Leserin, lieber Leser,

sicher zum Lernerfolg – mit Spaß und Spannung! Die Compact Lernkrimis mit ihrer Kombination aus Lektüre und didaktischem Übungsanteil eignen sich hervorragend, um breite Sprachkompetenzen in der Fremdsprache zu erwerben. Der Lerner wird dabei durch die spannende Handlung, das angemessene Sprachniveau und den stetig ansteigenden Schwierigkeitsgrad der Übungen gefördert und motiviert.

Entwickelt nach neuesten Erkenntnissen der Fremdsprachendidaktik, sind Compact Lernkrimis das ideale Medium für einen Lernerfolg im Selbststudium. Durch die kleinen Texteinheiten und den hohen Übungsanteil sind sie aber auch als Unterrichtslektüre bestens geeignet.

So lernen Sie mit Compact Lernkrimis:
- **Mit Begeisterung lernen:** Die packende Krimihandlung motiviert Sie beim Lesen des englischen Originaltextes.
- **Wissen intensivieren und erweitern:** Durch die Kombination aus didaktisierter Lektüre und textbezogenen Übungen testen und trainieren Sie Ihre Sprachkenntnisse effektiv. Vokabelangaben auf jeder Seite unterstützen Sie beim Lesen.
- **Systematisch lernen:** Knüpfen Sie an Ihr individuelles Sprachniveau an und setzen Sie eigene Lernziele – linear im Schwierigkeitsgrad ansteigend oder mit punktuellen Schwerpunkten von Grundwortschatz bis Hörverstehen.
- **Unabhängig sein:** Lernen Sie ganz individuell – wo und wann Sie wollen.

Viel Spaß beim spannend Englisch lernen
wünscht Ihnen

Prof. Dr. Christiane Neveling
Didaktik der romanischen Sprachen, Universität Leipzig

Inhalt

Zu diesem Buch

Das Mädcheninternat Shepton Mallet im beschaulichen Somerset feiert sein 100-jähriges Bestehen. Nach dem Fest verschwin-
det plötzlich eine ehemalige Schülerin und in ihrem zurückge-
lassenen Auto findet die Polizei Blutspuren. Wollte etwa jemand
aus dem Internat sie loswerden, oder ist der Anwältin einer ihrer
Fälle zum Verhängnis geworden?

Inspector Hudson und sein Team von Scotland Yard ermitteln
in Somerset, Birmingham und London, um die Vermisste zu
finden. Dabei stoßen sie auf Spuren, die weit in die Vergangen-
heit reichen. Denn in Shepton Mallet geschehen nicht zum ers-
ten Mal seltsame Dinge …

 The Open Day

It's a sunny Saturday morning in late July. In the beautiful little village of Shepton Mallet, [i] Henry, the school **caretaker** is working hard. Everything must look perfect before the guests arrive. He is hanging up a banner above the entrance. It says:

Shepton Mallet Boarding School, 1915 – 2015. 100 Years of Educating Girls!

"Very good, Henry," says a well-dressed, **middle-aged** woman, smiling. "Our **Open Day** will be a great **success**."

caretaker	Hausmeister
boarding school	Internat
to educate	(aus)bilden
middle-aged	mittleren Alters
open day	Tag der offenen Tür
success	Erfolg
stall	Verkaufsstand
handicrafts *pl*	Handarbeiten
head girl	Schulsprecherin
polite	höflich

She turns to a group of teenage girls. They all wear identical dark blue skirts, white shirts and blue and white ties.

"Now, Amy and Alice, you two set up the cake **stall** on the left of the garden, and Belinda, you can put up the **handicrafts** stall." She then turns to a tall girl with a ponytail.

"Joanna, your job as **head girl** is to welcome the guests. Be **polite** and charming."

"I'll do my best," Joanna says with a smile.

The woman smiles back at her.

> **Shepton Mallet** ist eine kleine Stadt im Südwesten Englands. Sie gehört zur Grafschaft Somerset, die bekannt ist für ihre schöne Landschaft und ihre Apfelplantagen.

Three hours later, the garden is full of guests. Women and girls of all ages are standing in little groups, many with their families. On one side of the garden a family is eating muffins and chatting.

to chat	sich unterhalten, plaudern
strict	streng
lazy	faul
curly	lockig
wedding	Hochzeit
That's a shame!	Wie schade!
to change the subject	das Thema wechseln
bossy	bestimmend, herrisch
prime minister	Premierminis- terin

"When I was a girl, the teachers were very strict," a white-haired lady tells her granddaughter. "If I was lazy in class, the teacher hit me on the back of the hand."

"Oh Granny, I don't believe you," laughs the little girl.

"It's true! Once I had to write 'I must not run in the corridor' one hundred times! Of course things are very different now."

"Hello and welcome. Would you like a glass of champagne?" asks Joanna, the head girl, with a charming smile.

"See what I mean?" says the grandmother. "Very different!"

On the other side of the garden, two old school friends say hello. One of the women has curly red hair and is wearing a colourful skirt. The other has short blonde hair and looks very business-like in a pencil skirt and blazer.

"Penny! How lovely to see you," says the red-haired woman. "You remember my husband, Brian, don't you?"

"Yes, Jennifer, of course. Hello Brian! Do you know, I haven't seen you both since your wedding," Penny replies.

> **Margaret Thatcher** war von 1979 bis 1990 Premierministerin des Vereinigten Königreichs. Sie war die erste und bislang einzige Frau in diesem Amt und berühmt für ihre oft unerbittliche Haltung, was ihr den Spitznamen „The Iron Lady" (die eiserne Dame) einbrachte.

"That's a long time ago," Jennifer laughs. "What about you? Where's your husband? Didn't he come with you today?"

"No, Neil is busy this weekend," answers Penny.

"That's a shame," says Jennifer. "You two are such a lovely couple. Penny, are you alright? You look rather tired."

"I'm fine. I've just got some stress at work at the moment," says Penny.

She quickly changes the subject.

Exercise 1: Adjectives. Lesen Sie weiter und unterstreichen Sie alle 9 Adjektive!

"Look at those uniforms, those lovely blue skirts," Penny says. "Do you remember our uniform when we were young?"

"My God, yes! Those ugly grey skirts and yellow blouses. We all looked terrible!" laughs Jennifer.

Just then Joanna walks past and offers them some champagne.

"Wow, things have changed here," says Jennifer when Joanna has gone. "Do you remember the head girl when we started?"

"You mean Margaret Taylor. I could never forget her. She was so bossy and arrogant – more like a prime minister[i] than a head girl."

"Yes, that's why we called her 'Thatcher' behind her back!" replies Jennifer, and both women start to laugh.

On the other side of the lawn, near the school gates, two women are standing watching the guests and smoking.

"Come on, Fiona. Let's go in," one of them says and **stubs out** her cigarette with the sole of her leather boot. "Don't you want to see how the others have changed?"

"Not really," says Fiona, lighting up another cigarette.

lawn	Rasen
gate	Tor
to stub out	ausdrücken
probably	wahrscheinlich
choir	Chor
assembly hall	Aula
peeping Tom	Spanner
binoculars *pl*	Fernglas
wood	kleiner Wald
to join in	mitmachen

"They're probably all rich, fat and boring."

Claire laughs. "You're terrible, Fi! They're not all bad."

A bell rings and the music teacher, Miss Wallis, appears.

"Ladies and gentlemen, we would like to invite you all to come inside. The school choir is about to sing in the assembly hall."

"Go on, Claire. I'll see you later at the Queen's Arms, okay?" Fiona turns to leave. "Claire, look over there. A peeping Tom!"

She points at a man on the other side of the gate. He is watching the school through binoculars.

The man sees her and moves away quickly towards the little wood behind the school. The two friends say goodbye and Claire walks up the path towards the huge stone building.

In the assembly hall, the choir sings the school song. Many of the women join in, some with tears in their eyes. This is too sentimental for Claire, so she goes out into the entrance hall. Here the walls are full of class photos from 1915 till the present year.

"Hello there!" says a voice beside her.

Claire looks up and sees a blonde woman in a business suit.

"Penny?" says Claire.

The woman nods. "Look, Claire. Here's our old class of 1985."
They both look closely at the photo of a group of 11-year-old
girls smiling at the camera-
man.

"And here's Miss Foster," says
Claire and points at the teach-
er standing beside the girls.
"She looks so young!"

"Years younger than we are
now," says Penny.

closely	genau
halfway human	halbwegs menschlich
to exclaim	ausrufen (Schock od. Überraschung)
row	Reihe

"I liked Miss Foster. What a shame she left the school."
"Yes," Claire replies, "she and Miss Musty were the only teachers
who were halfway human."

Exercise 2: Prepositions. Ergänzen Sie die Präpositionen!

above   at   behind   on   through

1. The teacher points _____ the blackboard.

2. She is looking out _____ the window.

3. The women are standing _____ the left side
   of the lawn.

4. The child is hiding _____ the curtain.

5. There is a banner hanging _____ the entrance.

"Oh Claire, look here!" Penny exclaims. "It's Becky."
She points at a little girl in the second row. This girl isn't smiling.
She is looking at the camera with a sad expression on her face.

"Do you ever think about what happened back then?"

"No, I try not to think about it. It was so sad," Claire replies.

truth	Wahrheit
suspicious of	misstrauisch gegenüber
crime	Verbrechen
lawyer	Anwältin
smart	*hier:* schick

"You know, I still don't really understand what happened that night," says Penny.

"There's nothing to understand. It was just a terrible accident."

"We were so young. Do you think they told us the whole truth? I sometimes think that they didn't."

"What do you mean?" asks Claire in surprise.

"Oh, it's just a feeling, probably nothing. My job makes me suspicious of everyone. I have too much to do with crime."

"Are you a policewoman?"

"No, I'm a lawyer," Penny replies.

So that explains the smart clothes, Claire thinks as she looks down at her own jeans and boots.

Exercise 3: True or false? Welche Aussagen sind korrekt? Markieren Sie mit richtig ✔ oder falsch – !

1. Penny and Claire were in the same class at school. ❒

2. Miss Foster was not a nice teacher. ❒

3. Becky was an unhappy child. ❒

4. Penny is now a policewoman. ❒

"Hello there! How lovely to see you after all these years."

The women turn round.

"Miss Musty! How are you?" asks Claire.

"Congratulations on your **promotion**," Penny says politely.

"I'm fine," says Miss Musty. "And thank you, Penny. I've been **headmistress** for 15

promotion	Beförderung
to retire	in Rente gehen
headmistress	Schulleiterin
Retirement Home	Altersheim

years now and I love it. And here's someone that you both know. You remember Margaret, don't you?"

A woman in an expensive-looking designer dress steps out from behind Miss Musty and says 'Hello'.

Claire and Penny smile at each other, both thinking "Thatcher!"

Exercise 4: Choose the correct alternative. Lesen Sie weiter und unterstreichen Sie die richtige Variante!

"Come on, ladies, let's **1.** getting / get a cup of tea," Miss Musty says, and she **2.** leads / is leading Claire, Penny and Margaret into the next room.

Here the school secretary **3.** is standing / stands at a long table set with cups and saucers. When they come in, she **4.** is pouring / pours them tea from a large teapot.

"Mrs Motherwell, how are you? I didn't know you still work here," says Margaret.

"I'm very well, thank you, my dear. Yes, I'm still here, until I **retire** in a couple of years. Would you like sugar in your tea?"

"What happened to Miss Sharp after she retired?" asks Penny.

"She still lives in Shepton Mallet," replies Miss Musty. "At the Sunshine **Retirement Home** on the other side of the village."

11

"**My goodness**, I can't **imagine** Miss Sharp in an old people's home. I **bet** they're all afraid of her!" says Claire, half joking. Miss Musty laughs. "Yes, she was a very strict headmistress."
"So what are you all doing now?" asks Margaret.

My goodness!	Meine Güte!
to imagine	sich vorstellen
to bet	wetten
Foreign Office *UK*	Außenministe-rium
to stay in touch	in Kontakt bleiben
business card	Visitenkarte
to sigh	seufzen
pale	blass

But before anyone can reply, she tells them what she is doing. "I'm at the **Foreign Office**. Terribly busy, of course. And I have to travel all the time. It was difficult while the children were young. But luckily they are both very clever. Adrian is studying at Oxford now and Prunella is a medical student at St. Thomas' Hospital."

Penny and Claire give each other a quick look, both thinking the same thing.

"This is such fun – meeting up again after so long," says Margaret. "We must **stay in touch**. Here, take these," she says, handing Penny and Claire two shiny **business cards**.

"Wait a second," says Penny, searching through her handbag. Eventually[i] she finds her business cards at the bottom of her bag under her mobile phone and gives them to the others. At that moment they hear the start of Beethoven's Fifth Symphony coming from Penny's handbag. She takes her phone out of her bag, looks at the display and **sighs**.

False friends alarm!
eventually heißt „endlich, schließlich" und nicht „eventuell", was man mit **maybe** oder **perhaps** übersetzt.

"Excuse me," she says nervously and goes outside.

Minutes later she returns. She looks **pale**.
"Are you alright, Penny?" asks Miss Musty. "You look worried."

"It's just a problem at work," Penny replies. She turns her phone off. "That's better. Now I won't be **disturbed** again." She smiles at the others. "Sorry, what were you saying, Margaret?"

| to disturb | stören |

Exercise 5: Pronouns. Ersetzen Sie die markierten Wörter durch die entsprechenden Pronomen!

1. Margaret gives **Penny and Claire** her business card.

   _____

2. Penny searches for **her mobile phone** in her bag.

   _____

3. Claire can't imagine **Miss Sharp** in an old people's home.

   _____

4. **Margaret's children** are both very clever.

   _____

It's early evening now and the guests are starting to leave.
"Are you driving back to Birmingham tonight?" asks Claire.
"No," Penny answers. "I'm staying overnight at the White Hart. You know, the hotel next to the pub."
"Me too. Let's walk back together. Are you ready to leave?"
"Let me just say goodbye to Jennifer," says Penny.
"I'll wait for you outside," says Claire and walks into the garden. It's quiet there now. She smokes a cigarette while she waits. Suddenly she hears a noise on the other side of the school gate.

It's the man with the binoculars again! He's *still* watching the school! **What on earth** does he want? thinks Claire.

What on earth...!	Was zum Teufel...?!
startled	erschrocken
to tap	klopfen, tippen
churchyard	Friedhof
in silence	schweigend
⚡ teacher's pet	Lehrers Liebling, Streberin
to oversleep	verschlafen

"Hey, you! What are you doing?" The man looks **startled**. He runs to a dark-coloured coupé parked by the gate and drives off. A minute later Penny **taps** her on the shoulder and now Claire is startled.

"Are you alright, Claire? I heard you shout."

Claire tells Penny about the peeping Tom.

"Well, there's no one there now, so let's go," says Penny, and they walk through the village towards the hotel.

It's getting dark as they pass a little church. They both turn to look at the **churchyard** and then walk on **in silence** until they arrive at the Queen's Arms pub next to the hotel.

"I'm meeting Fiona here," says Claire. "Do you want to join us?"

"No, I don't think so," answers Penny.

"Wait a minute. I'll just send Fiona a text message to tell her I'm here."

While Claire writes her message, Penny turns her phone back on. It beeps loudly several times. "Oh no, not more messages."

A woman with long black hair and wearing a leather jacket and jeans comes out of the pub and walks towards them.

"Hi Fiona! Look, I've brought Penny with me," says Claire.

"Hello Penny," says Fiona coldly.

"Hello Fiona," Penny replies without smiling. "Look, Claire, I'm tired, so I'm going to my room now. Let's meet for breakfast tomorrow around 8:30, okay?"

The other two watch as she walks quickly towards the hotel.

It's a warm evening, so Fiona and Claire sit in the beer garden.

"Guess who was at the Open Day – Thatcher! And she's got this perfect life...it makes you sick!" Claire says.

"What about Miss Penelope, teacher's pet?" asks Fiona. "Is she still perfect, too?"

"Penny's a lawyer now. If you ask me, she's a workaholic. Her phone never stops ringing. And she is always thinking about crime. Do you know, she even told me she thinks there was something suspicious about that accident in 1985."

Fiona listens with interest. "Penny always was the cleverest girl in the class," she says.

Exercise 6: Unscramble the words. Lesen Sie weiter und bringen Sie die Buchstaben in die richtige Reihenfolge!

It's Sunday **1.** norgmin _____ and Claire is sitting in the breakfast room at the White Hart Hotel. She looks at her **2.** chawt _____: 9 a.m. That's funny, she **3.** kinsth _____. Penny is always on time. **4.** sherapp _____ she has **overslept**. She waits another 10 minutes and then goes to the **5.** porceeiont _____.

"Could you please call Mrs Sutton and tell her I'm waiting for her."

"Mrs Sutton has already checked out," answers the receptionist.

"Are you sure? We wanted to meet for breakfast."

"Yes, madam. She left early this morning, before I was **on duty**."

"How **strange**! So you didn't see her?"

"No. She just left the money and keys on the desk. And a note saying she had to get back to work."

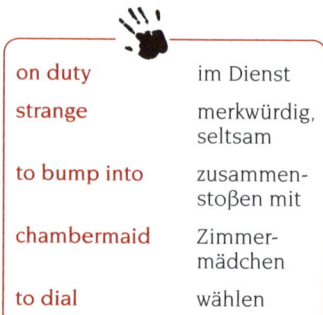

on duty	im Dienst
strange	merkwürdig, seltsam
to bump into	zusammen-stoßen mit
chambermaid	Zimmer-mädchen
to dial	wählen

Poor Penny, her job must be very stressful. As Claire turns to walk back to the breakfast room to finish her coffee, she **bumps into** a **chambermaid**. She has come from cleaning the bedrooms.

"Look, Michele," she says to the receptionist, "I found this in room 14." And she puts a mobile phone on the desk.

Exercise 7: Question and answer. Beantworten Sie die Fragen zur Geschichte!

1. Who is Miss Musty?

   _____

2. Where does Claire meet Fiona after the Open Day?

   _____

3. Why doesn't Fiona like Penny?

   _____

4. Where does the chambermaid find Penny's phone?

   _____

"Room 14 you say, Sharon? That was Mrs Sutton's room. Miss Hockey?" she calls after Claire. "It seems Mrs Sutton left her mobile phone here. Do you know how we can contact her?"

"Possibly. One moment," Claire says.

She gets out the business card that Penny gave her the day before. The number of 'Corbett & Co Lawyers Ltd' is written on it, but also what looks like a private number. Claire dials this number and hears it ring several times. Then she hears Penny's voice: "Neil and I are not at home, so please leave a message."

"Penny, it's Claire here. It's a shame you had to leave so early. It was nice seeing you again. Listen, you left your phone at the White Hart. Call me back. Bye!"

The Red Toyota

It's 10 p.m. on Monday evening. Sergeant Wilson and PC O'Malley are driving through Brixton❶ in their squad car.

"Mondays are boring, aren't they, sir?" comments O'Malley. "It's so quiet. Everyone's home watching the football match on TV."

"Yeah, but it's better than working at the weekend," says Wilson. They come to a green light and start to cross.

"Watch out, sir!" shouts O'Malley as a car suddenly comes speeding from the right and nearly hits them.

Wilson immediately switches on the blue light and starts to follow the car. O'Malley picks up the walkie-talkie to contact the police station.

PC (police constable)	Polizeibeamter/in
squad car	Streifenwagen
to speed	rasen
accelerator	Gaspedal
to overtake	überholen
fence	Zaun
case	Fall
to arrest	festnehmen
to joyride	eine Spritztour machen
scrapyard	Schrottplatz
to trace	aufspüren

"PC O'Malley here. We're following a red Toyota down Stockwell Road. It crossed at a red light and nearly hit us. Now it's speeding up. The driver is trying to get away."

Wilson puts his foot down on the accelerator. Soon the police car is right behind the Toyota and starts to overtake. The driver of the Toyota panics, loses control and crashes into a large metal fence by the side of the road.

"We've got them!" says O'Malley into his walkie talkie.
Wilson stops the squad car. The two policemen get out and walk over to the wreck.
"Get out and put your hands up!" shouts Wilson.
The car doors open slowly. The driver and passengers get out.
"Well, look at that! It's just a group of kids," says PC O'Malley.

Exercise 8: Verb forms. Lesen Sie weiter und setzen Sie die korrekte Verbform ein!

It **1.** be _____ early Tuesday morning at Scotland Yard. Inspector Hudson **2.** knock _____ on Sir Reginald's door and goes inside.

"Morning James, I've got a new **case** for you. Last night two of our officers in Brixton **arrested** a group of teenagers. They **3.** be _____ **joyriding** in a stolen car. The teenagers are from Basingstoke.[i] They say they **4.** find _____ the car at a **scrapyard** there and **5.** think _____ it would be fun to drive it up to London."

"But joyriding isn't a job for Scotland Yard," Hudson replies. "It's not that simple. Our men in Brixton have **traced** the car's owner – a Mrs Penelope Sutton," Sir Reginald explains.

Brixton ist ein Stadtbezirk von London. Er liegt südlich der Stadtmitte und ist ein sozialer Brennpunkt.
Basingstoke liegt auf halber Strecke zwischen Brixton und Somerset.

"Have they spoken to Mrs Sutton yet?"

"No. They found her business card in the car and tried to call her. No one answered at her private number so they rang her work number – a law firm in Birmingham. The secretary told them Mrs Sutton was in Somerset at the weekend. She was staying at the White Hart Hotel in Shepton Mallet. They expected her at work yesterday, but she didn't come."

"So Mrs Sutton is missing," says Hudson.

"Yes," Sir Reginald replies. "Sergeant Wilson and PC O'Malley searched the car, looking for drugs."

"Did they find any?" asks Hudson.

"No," replies Sir Reginald. "But when they opened the car boot, they found a lot of blood. I'm afraid Mrs Sutton may be the victim of a violent crime."

law firm	Anwaltskanzlei
to expect	erwarten
car boot	Kofferraum
victim	Opfer
violent crime	Gewaltverbrechen
database	Datenbank
recent	aktuell
next-of-kin	nächster Angehörige
straight away	sofort
denim jacket	Jeansjacke

"Listen, everyone," says Hudson. "A woman called Mrs Penelope Sutton is missing and she may be in danger. Harvey, put Mrs Sutton's name in the national database of missing persons. And find out what you can about her background. I need a recent photo of her and the name of her next-of-kin."

"Yes, sir!" says Constable Harvey.

She is young and very enthusiastic about her job. She starts working straight away.

Hudson turns to a man with round glasses and a denim jacket. "Bradley, I want you to go to the scrapyard in Basingstoke."

"A scrapyard in Basingstoke?" DI Joe Bradley asks. He doesn't sound very enthusiastic.

"Yes, that's where the teenagers found Mrs Sutton's car.
The **forensic** team is already
searching for **clues** there.
Your job is to question the
owner of the scrapyard. Find
out if he saw who left the car

forensic	gerichtsmedi-zinisch
clue	Hinweis
suspicious	verdächtig
shoulder-length	schulterlang
jealous	neidisch

there. And ask people around the area of the scrapyard if they
saw anything **suspicious**."

"Yes, sir," says Bradley quietly.

"We already know that Mrs Sutton lives in Birmingham. She
works for a law firm in Pritchett Street," says Hudson.

Next he turns to a young woman with **shoulder-length** brown
hair.

"Jarvis, I want you to go to Birmingham. Talk to Mrs Sutton's boss
and colleagues. Maybe they have an idea where she might be."

"It sounds like an interesting case, sir," says DI Wendy Jarvis.

Bradley gives her a **jealous** look.

Exercise 9: Match-up. Welche der folgenden Begriffe
gehören zusammen? Ordnen Sie zu!

1. ☐ next-of-   **a)** firm
2. ☐ car   **b)** crime
3. ☐ law   **c)** kin
4. ☐ violent   **d)** boot

"Excuse me, sir. I've found Mrs Sutton's home address and her
husband's mobile phone number," says Constable Harvey.

"Thank you, Harvey. Jarvis, go to this address. Talk to Mr Sutton and say you want to search his house. If he won't help you, get a **search warrant**. Look for any clues – anything that explains why Mrs Sutton has **disappeared**. And ask the Birmingham police force to send you an assistant to help."

search warrant	Durchsuchungs-befehl
to disappear	verschwinden
to frown	die Stirn runzeln
to examine	untersuchen
to compare	vergleichen
to be in charge	die Verantwor-tung tragen
Constabulary	Polizeirevier

"No problem, sir," says DI Jarvis with a smile.

Bradley **frowns**. He didn't give *me* an assistant, he thinks.

"Dr Barrington is already **examining** Mrs Sutton's car," Hudson continues. "Jarvis, while you're at the Suttons' house, try to find something that the forensic team can use to **compare** the DNA with the blood in the car, like a toothbrush or a hairbrush."

Jarvis smiles and nods.

Hudson turns to the others. "I'm driving to Somerset – to the hotel where Mrs Sutton spent the weekend – to talk to the people who saw her last. While I'm gone, I'd like you, Harvey, to be **in charge** of things in the office. You can ask Sir Reginald to give you an assistant if you need any help. Do you think you can manage?"

"Oh yes, sir! Thank you, sir!" says Harvey, giving him a big smile. "I'll certainly do my best."

Even *she* gets an assistant! Bradley thinks angrily.

"And Harvey, can you also let the Somerset **Constabulary** know that I'm coming," Hudson tells her. "I may need their help with the case. Remember, team, we must all work quickly. A woman's life is in danger."

It's 12:30 midday. Hudson is sitting in a motorway cafe on the M3. ⓘ

"Sir, I've spoken to the police in Somerset," says Harvey on the phone. "Inspector Matthews at the station in Warminster is your contact. He sounds quite excited about working with you." She gives Hudson the number and rings off.

Hudson reads through his notes on the Sutton case. This will be an interesting job, he thinks. But it means I'll be away from home for a while. I should tell Miss Paddington. He picks up his mobile and dials his home number in London.

excited	aufgeregt, begeistert
to be just about to	gerade dabei sein, etw. zu tun
shepherd's pie	Auflauf mit Lammfleisch und Kartoffelbrei
housekeeper	Haushälterin
emergency	Notfall
investigation	Ermittlung

"Hello, it's James here."

"James, I was just about to call you. I'm cooking shepherd's pie this evening. What time will you be home for dinner?"

"Miss Paddington, I'm afraid I'm not coming home this evening. I've got a new case. I'm on my way to Somerset right now. I'm staying at a hotel there tonight, and maybe for longer, too."

"Oh James, you always work so hard. Have you got everything you need?" his housekeeper asks in a motherly voice.

"Yes, don't worry about me," he says. "I've got my emergency overnight bag. If the investigation goes on for long, I'll come home and get some fresh clothes."

ⓘ Der M3 motorway, die Autobahn M3, verläuft durch die englischen Grafschaften Hampshire und Surrey südwestlich von London.
Das Tempolimit auf Autobahnen ist 70 miles per hour, ca. 113 km/h.

"Alright, James. Good luck with the case. You can tell me all about it when you get home!" Miss Paddington ends the call.

Exercise 10: Correct the mistakes. Lesen Sie weiter und korrigieren Sie die sechs Fehler!

DI Joe Bradley standing in the middle of a scrapyard in Basingstoke. He sighs. Why does Hudson always gives the most interesting jobs to Jarvis? Next to him stands a 14-years-old boy wearing lot of hair gel and rings threw his eyebrows. He is busy writing a message on his handy.

1. _____
2. _____
3. _____
4. _____
5. _____
6. _____

"Shane, stop that now," says Bradley **impatiently**. "Show me exactly where you found the car."

"Over there, **mate**," replies the boy. "Next to the wrecks."

Bradley and the boy walk over to a **pile** of wrecked cars at the side of the yard. Here three forensic officers in **protective clothing** are searching for clues.

"What did you do next?" asks Bradley.

"The car looked great," says Shane. "And the door wasn't locked. So I said to my mates, '**Let's take her for a spin!**'"

"So you drove out through the gates over there?"

"Past the train station and onto the M3!" says the boy **proudly**.

"Did you see anyone else in the scrapyard?"

Shane shakes his head. "It was very late. The place was empty."

"Hey, you! How long will this take?" An old man with white hair and a **wrinkled** face comes over to Bradley. "I don't like this. There are police all over my yard!" He takes his cigarette out of his mouth and spits on the ground angrily.

Bradley sighs again. "I already told you, Mr Dawkins. This is a crime scene now. Did you see who left the car here?"

"No, I never saw a red Toyota. It wasn't here when I left on Friday evening to go to the Dog and Duck. And it wasn't here on Monday morning when I came back to work. "

"You left the gates open all weekend, didn't you? Don't you ever lock up?" asks Bradley.

impatiently	ungeduldig
⚡ mate	Kumpel
pile	Haufen
protective clothing	Schutzbekleidung
Let's take her for a spin.	Lass uns eine Spritztour machen.
proudly	stolz
wrinkled	runzelig
to spit	spuken
crime scene	Tatort
to lock up	abschließen
factory	Fabrik
security guard	Sicherheits-bediensteter
meanwhile	währenddessen

"There's nothing here to steal," replies Dawkins.

"Wait here, Shane. I'm going to have a look around," says Bradley. He walks out of the scrapyard and along the street outside. Next to the scrapyard is a small factory. Bradley walks up to the entrance and waves at a security guard behind the gate.

"Detective Inspector Bradley," he shouts and holds out his ID card. "I'm investigating a crime at the scrapyard next door. Can I ask you a few questions?"

Meanwhile in Edgbaston, an expensive part of Birmingham, DI Jarvis walks up the path to the Suttons' home. With her is a young police officer from the Birmingham Constabulary. She rings the doorbell and waits, but there is no answer.

Englische Pubs haben oft eher traditionelle Namen wie **The Crown,** oder **The King's Head,** aber es gibt auch lustige Beispiele wie **The Pig and Whistle, The Hairy Lemon** oder **The Mad Dog.**

1. Notfall ___ ___ ___ ___ ___ ___ [ ] ___

2. Haufen ___ ___ [ ] ___

3. stolz ___ ___ ___ [ ] ___

4. Nachricht ___ [ ] ___ ___ ___ ___ ___

Lösung: [ ][ ][ ][ ]

"Shall I break the door down, Inspector?" asks Constable Cavanagh in an excited voice.

"You watch too many action films, I think!" says Jarvis, amused. She takes out her phone and dials the mobile number for Mr Sutton, Penny's husband.

"Neil here," says a deep voice.

"Mr Sutton, this is Detective Inspector Jarvis from Scotland Yard. I need to contact your wife **urgently**. Can you tell me where she is?"

"How should I know where Penny is? She hasn't spoken to me for over two weeks," he replies in a loud and angry voice.

"So you don't live together?"

"No. She **kicked me out**! She says we need some time apart."ⓘ

"Well, I'm afraid your wife is missing," Jarvis tells him **gently**. Sutton doesn't reply.

"Mr Sutton? Are you still there?" Jarvis asks.

"Penny... missing?" he says quietly.

"We need your help to find your wife. I'm standing outside your house right now. Can you come and let us in?"

"Yes, of course," says Mr Sutton. "I'll be there in ten minutes."

urgently	dringend
to kick sb. out	jmd. rausschmeißen
gently	sanft
surrounded by	umgeben von
oak	Eiche
to gasp	nach Luft schnappen, kurz einatmen
to wonder	sich fragen
to sign	unterschreiben

Hudson looks at his watch. It's 1:30 p.m. It was a three-hour journey from London to Shepton Mallet. He parks his car outside the White Hart Hotel, an old black and white building **surrounded by** large **oak** trees. Next to it is a pretty little pub with roses around the door. Hudson walks into the hotel's reception area.

"How can I help you, sir?" asks Michele, the receptionist, politely.

"Hudson, Scotland Yard," he says, holding out his ID card. I'm investigating the case of a missing person – Penelope Sutton."

Michele **gasps**. "Mrs Sutton, you say? She's missing?"

Hudson nods. "Tell me everything you know."

"She stayed here last Saturday night, in room 14. But she went home very early on Sunday morning, even before I was on duty."

"What time do you start work?" asks Hudson.

"7 a.m.," replies Michele.

"That is very early for a Sunday morning. I **wonder** why she left so soon. Did she say anything to you the day before?"

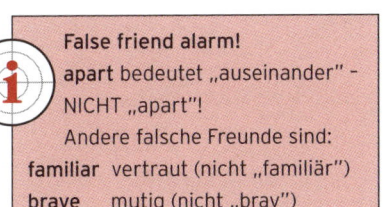

False friend alarm!
apart bedeutet „auseinander" – NICHT „apart"!
Andere falsche Freunde sind:
familiar vertraut (nicht „familiär")
brave mutig (nicht „brav")

"No," says Michele, "but I found this on my desk." She passes him a little hand-written note. Hudson reads it: *Emergency at work. Must leave early.* The note is **signed** Penelope Sutton.

"And the chambermaid found this in her room." Michele hands him Penny's mobile phone.

"Thank you," says Hudson. He puts the note and the phone in his pocket. "Can I have the keys to her room, please?"

"Oh, we have a new guest staying there at the moment," Michele replies. "But I'll ask him for you. I'm sure it will be okay."

"Excuse me," says a voice behind him. "I heard you say that you are looking for Penny. Is she in trouble?"

Hudson turns and sees a woman of about forty with short red hair.

"Claire Hockey," she says and holds out her hand. "I was at school with Penny."

| upset | aufgebracht |

Hudson shakes her hand. "Is there a quiet place where we can talk?" he asks.

Claire leads him into the empty breakfast room.

An hour later, Hudson is sitting alone in the hotel lounge drinking a cup of tea. I didn't find any clues in room 14, he thinks sadly. The chambermaid did her job too well. But Miss Hockey was helpful. He reads the notes he made during his talk with Claire:

school open day... met old friends, e.g. Jennifer Blacksmith, Margaret Taylor, headmistress Veronica Musty

– I will have to talk to all of them, he thinks –

Penny upset about a phone call... strange man watching school through binoculars... Drives off in dark-coloured coupé...

That sounds very suspicious...

Miss Hockey last saw Penny outside Queen's Arms where she was meeting her friend, Fiona Lambert, at 7 p.m.

So I've got a lot of people to interview, thinks Hudson. I'll start with Miss Musty at the school.

Exercise 12: Opposites. Verbinden Sie die Gegenteile!

1. ☐ rudely
2. ☐ happily
3. ☐ badly
4. ☐ aggressively

a) sadly
b) politely
c) gently
d) well

Mr Sutton **unlocks** the front door of his house in Edgbaston.
"Please wait here, sir, while we search the house," says Jarvis.
He nods and stands outside alone, looking **miserable**.
"You start upstairs and I'll do the ground floor," Jarvis tells Cavanagh as she picks up a pile of post and newspapers from the mat inside the front door.

She walks from room to room looking for clues. Everything is very **neat and tidy**. There's no **sign** of a fight. Jarvis sees a large collection of CDs sorted in alphabetical order. B for Bizet... C for Chopin... They really like classical music, she thinks.

to unlock	aufschließen
miserable	elend
neat and tidy	ordentlich, pico-bello
sign	Zeichen, Hinweis
windowsill	Fensterbank
wooden	aus Holz
court	*hier*: Gericht

Next she goes into the kitchen. It's a sunny room with flowers on the **windowsill**. Jarvis finds two letters on the big **wooden** table.
She picks one up and reads:
Invitation to Shepton Mallet School Open Day, July 18th
She then looks at the other letter. It's from the **court**.

In Wohnhäusern wird die Post meistens durch einen Schlitz in der Eingangstür geliefert.

*A date has been set for the case of Wiley **versus** Wiley – August 3rd, 2015.*

Jarvis puts both letters in her pocket.

"Cavanagh, how are you doing?" she shouts.

The constable comes down the stairs carrying a plastic

versus	gegen
evidence	Beweis
liar	Lügner
appointment	Termin
to get one's hands on sb.	jmd. in die Finger kriegen
CU (see you)	wir sehen uns
outgoing calls *pl*	ausgehende Anrufe

evidence bag. "I found a pink toothbrush in the bathroom," he says proudly.

"Good. I'll send that to Dr Barrington straight away. Let's go."

As they leave they see Mr Sutton still waiting on the doorstep.

"Do you know anything about this, Mr Sutton?" asks Jarvis and shows him the letter about the open day.

"Yes," he says, looking very pale. "Penny told me about her school open day last time I saw her. But I really have no idea why she didn't come home. Detective, will you please let me know if there is any news?"

"Of course, sir. And please call me at this number if your wife contacts you." Jarvis gives him her card.

"Do you think he kidnapped her?" asks Cavanagh when the two officers are in their car.

"No, he really does look very worried about her, doesn't he?" Jarvis replies.

"Maybe he's just a good liar. I saw a film once..."

"Yes, thank you, Cavanagh! Let's go now please!"

And so they drive towards the

bloody bedeutet zwar "blutig", es ist aber auch ein häufig verwendetes Schimpfwort, abgeleitet vom Ausruf „By my Lady!" (Jungfrau Maria). Deshalb sollte man ein blutiges Steak als „rare steak" und nicht als „bloody steak" (verdammtes Steak) übersetzen!

city centre and Corbett & Co Lawyers Ltd.

Exercise 13: Contracted forms. Lesen Sie weiter und ergänzen Sie die Kurzformen!

My appointment with Miss Musty is in 90 minutes, thinks Hudson. So **1.** I have _____ got time to have a look at the village. While **2.** he is _____ walking, he listens to the voice mail on Penny's phone.

"You bloody[i] bitch! **3.** You are _____ ruining my life!" says a man's voice.

Charming! thinks Hudson and clicks to the next message.

4. It is _____ from the same number.

"If I get my hands on you, **5.** you will _____ wish you were dead!"

Very interesting indeed, thinks Hudson. He takes out his own phone and calls Scotland Yard.

"Harvey, I want you to trace a mobile phone number. It's 0776 2341 4297. Thanks, bye."

He pauses under an oak tree to look at Penny's text messages. There are three from Saturday evening, all from a sender with the number 085 7825 6679. He reads them carefully:

8 p.m.: `1985: A pack of lies!`

8:25 p.m.: `Ask HM`; and finally at 8:45 p.m.:

`CU at QA in 10 minutes.`

"Harvey, it's me again. I need you to trace another number, too."

Next he checks Penny's outgoing calls. She only made one call last Saturday, at 8:35 p.m. Hudson redials the number.

"Sunshine Retirement Home, Sarah speaking," says a friendly woman's voice.

"Detective Inspector Hudson here. Did you receive a call from a Mrs Sutton on Saturday evening?"

"Yes, she wanted to know our visiting hours for the next day."

"Who did she want to visit on Sunday?" asks Hudson.

"I don't know, she didn't say. And she never came."

DI Jarvis is sitting in Penny's boss's office in central Birmingham. "No, I'm sorry, Inspector, I don't know where Penelope is. She hasn't come to work since last Friday," says a **bald** man with a grey **moustache** and a **bow tie**.

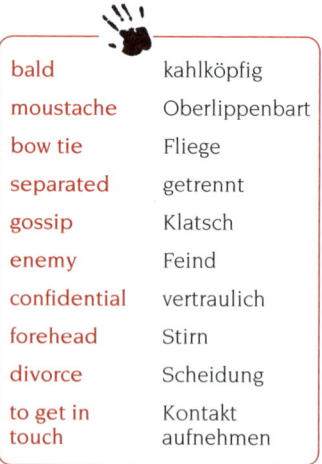

bald	kahlköpfig
moustache	Oberlippenbart
bow tie	Fliege
separated	getrennt
gossip	Klatsch
enemy	Feind
confidential	vertraulich
forehead	Stirn
divorce	Scheidung
to get in touch	Kontakt aufnehmen

"This is serious, I'm afraid, Mr Corbett. Mrs Sutton may be in danger. If you know anything at all, please tell me. Did she have any personal problems?" Jarvis asks.

"Well, I heard that she and her husband are **separated**. But I don't know all the **gossip**. Maybe you should ask Mrs Lovett, our secretary. She always knows everything that's going on."

"Yes, I'll speak to her later. What about work? Did Mrs Sutton have any problems there? Was anyone aggressive towards her?"

"You know, lawyers always have **enemies**. It's part of the job," he replies. "But I never thought Penelope was in danger."

"What can you tell me about this?" asks Jarvis, putting a letter on the table. "Wiley versus Wiley".

"I can't tell you about our clients, Inspector. That's **confidential** information."

After a few more minutes, Jarvis says goodbye and walks out of Mr Corbett's office. She feels frustrated.

I need to find out more about the Wiley case, she thinks.

In the reception area, Cavanagh is drinking coffee with Mrs Lovett, the secretary, a smartly dressed blonde. Mrs Lovett gives Jarvis a friendly smile.

"Your colleague here told me you're trying to find Penelope?"

Jarvis nods. "Yes, that's right."

"Let me know if I can help in any way," continues Mrs Lovett.

Jarvis smiles back and goes outside to phone Hudson.

"Hello, sir, it's Jarvis here. I've just spoken to Mrs Sutton's boss. But he won't give me any information about the Wiley case."

"Maybe he will when you tell him this," replies Hudson. "Harvey has traced the number of the aggressive phone calls. They came from Mr Ted Wiley."

"Bingo!" says Jarvis. "I'll talk to Corbett again right away!"

She goes back inside. The secretary and Cavanagh both look up.

"I need to speak to your boss again, Mrs Lovett."

"I'll see what I can do," she replies and picks up her phone. "Mr Corbett, the Police Inspector is still here. She needs to talk to you again." She smiles at Jarvis. "You can go in now, dear."

"Mr Corbett, we've got some new information. We now know that Mr Wiley sent Mrs Sutton some very aggressive messages. We're worried about her. We must speak to Wiley as soon as possible. Now what can you tell me about that case, Wiley versus Wiley?"

Corbett sighs and rubs his forehead. "OK, I'll tell you everything I know. What's important now is that you find Penelope quickly."

He takes a deep breath and goes on. "Wiley's wife, Brenda, is Penelope's client. Mrs Wiley wants a divorce, but her husband doesn't. He's a violent man and he beats her."

"Thank you, Mr Corbett. How can I get in touch with the Wileys?"

intercom	Gegensprechanlage
recently	in letzter Zeit
it's not like her	es ist nicht ihre Art

"One moment. Mrs Lovett?" Corbett speaks into an **intercom**. "Please find the address for Mr and Mrs Wiley. Goodbye, Inspector Jarvis. And good luck!"

In the reception area Mrs Lovett gives Jarvis the address of the Wileys' house in Dudley, a town 10 miles south of Birmingham.

"But you won't find Mrs Wiley there," she tells Jarvis. "Penelope told me she moved out three weeks ago."

"Do you have any idea where she is?" asks Jarvis.

"Yes," says Mrs Lovett with a smile. "Brenda Wiley is staying at her sister's house in Solihull. Here's the address."

"Where do you think Mrs Sutton might be?" asks Jarvis.

"Well, I know Penelope is having some problems with her husband, Neil. They're a lovely couple, but they've had some very bad arguments **recently**. Have you spoken to him yet?"

"Yes, we have. He says he has no idea where his wife is."

"I hope she's okay. **It's not like her** to miss work without calling me. I'm very worried about her, Inspector."

Exercise 14: Relationship matching. Ergänzen Sie die fehlenden Begriffe!

assistant   boss   husband   colleague

1. DI Jarvis is DI Bradley's _____.
2. Mr Sutton is Penny's _____.
3. PC Cavanagh is DI Jarvis's _____.
4. Mr Corbett is Penny's _____.

3 The Teacher's Pet

"This is Mr Brown," says the factory manager in Basingstoke. "He was here at the weekend. Talk to him."

DI Bradley turns to a young man with long hair and a beard. "So you're the night-watchman, Mr Brown?"

"Yeah, that's me. It's a good job – no early mornings," he grins.

night-watchman	Nachtwächter
CCTV (closed-circuit television)	Überwachungskamera

"Did you see anything strange at the scrapyard at the weekend?"

"No. I'm not paid to watch the scrapyard. That would cost extra!"

Bradley sighs. He leaves the factory and walks up and down the street to clear his mind. I'm getting nowhere, he thinks. He stops and looks around him. Then he sees it – a CCTV camera on the factory wall! It's pointing towards the street outside the factory, the same street that leads to the scrapyard.

"I've got the contact information you wanted for Jennifer Blacksmith, Margaret Taylor and Fiona Lambert, sir," says PC Harvey. "Blacksmith lives in Bath and Taylor in London. Mrs Lambert's address is in Shepton Mallet, not far from the school."

She gives him the addresses and phone numbers.

"Thank you, Harvey," says Hudson and smiles. She's doing well. I'm glad I gave her this chance to show that she's good at her job. "And I traced the text messages that Mrs Sutton received, too. They were from Fiona Lambert."

Hudson looks at his watch. Still 30 minutes before I meet Miss Musty. Time to visit Mrs Lambert. He opens a map of Shepton Mallet on his mobile phone and walks towards Fiona's house.

Meanwhile at the White Hart Hotel, Fiona knocks on Claire's door.

⚡ What's up?	Was ist los?
to be in a terrible hurry	es schrecklich eilig haben
Never mind.	Macht nichts.
weeds	Unkraut
to mow the lawn	Rasen mähen
to move out	ausziehen
state	Zustand

"**What's up**, Fiona? You're really pale. Are you ill?"

Fiona shakes her head. "Is it true about Penny?" she asks. "That she's disappeared and the police are looking for her?"

"Yes, she didn't come to breakfast on Sunday. She checked herself out really early. She **was in a terrible hurry**, it seems. She even left her phone behind," says Claire.

Exercise 15: Translation. Übersetzen Sie die folgenden Sätze!

1. What's up?

_____

2. She's doing well.

_____

3. Never mind!

_____

4. I'm getting nowhere!

_____

"Where's her phone now?" she asks, going even paler.
"The Inspector from London has got it. He's probably checking all her calls," Claire tells her friend.

Hudson arrives at Fiona's house in Shepton Mallet. He rings the doorbell and waits. There's no one home. **Never mind,** I'll try again later. But now it's time for my meeting with Miss Musty, the headmistress of Shepton Mallet School.

At the same time in Dudley, DI Jarvis and PC Cavanagh arrive at Mr and Mrs Wiley's house. All the curtains are closed and there is no sign of life. Jarvis knocks on the door but there's no answer. "Damn, there's no one home," she says. "Let's check the back." Behind the house is a small garden. The grass is long and full of **weeds**. Over in the next garden, a man is **mowing his lawn**. "Hello!" shouts Jarvis. "Do you know where Mr Wiley is?"

Exercise 16: Verb forms. Lesen Sie weiter und setzen Sie die korrekte Verbform ein!

The man **1. turn off** _____ his lawnmower and **2. walk** _____ towards her.
"Ted? No idea," he **3. reply** _____. "I haven't seen him since last Thursday. And Brenda **moved out**, poor woman. That's why the garden **4. be** _____ in such a bad **state**."
"Thank you. Okay, Cavanagh, let's **5. go** _____ and talk to Mrs Wiley," says Jarvis.

At 4:30 p.m. on Tuesday, Hudson walks up the path to Shepton Mallet School, a huge stone building with a big garden around it. A traditional public school,[i] thinks Hudson.

A man with thick grey hair and work clothes walks past him slowly, pushing a wheelbarrow.

"Good afternoon," says Hudson politely.

The man stares at him but he doesn't reply.

"Hello, you must be Inspector Hudson," says Miss Musty as she comes out to greet him. She looks very smart in her green silk blouse and skirt. "Don't worry about Henry.

He's been working at the school for a long time. He's a very good gardener but not a good talker," she says and laughs. "Let's go inside."

She leads Hudson into the school and along a corridor. They walk past a room where a woman with curly grey hair and glasses is busy typing a letter.

"Mrs Motherwell, please bring us some tea," says Miss Musty to her secretary. She takes Hudson into her office next door.

"Please take a seat," says Miss Musty. "How can I help you?"

"I am trying to find a missing person – a Mrs Penelope Sutton," Hudson explains.

Miss Musty looks blank.

"Her maiden name was Braithwaite," Hudson adds.

"Ah, Penny! Yes, she was a pupil here back in the 80s. I taught her French. She had a terrible accent! She was here on Saturday for the open day... What do you mean, 'a missing person'?"

"No one has seen Mrs Sutton since Saturday, I'm afraid. I need to find out exactly what she did that day."

"Of course, Inspector. I'll do my best to help you. Poor Penny! I wonder where she is." Miss Musty looks very worried.

"Tell me, how was Mrs Sutton when you saw her?"

"She was fine. She's a successful lawyer now. I'm so proud of her. She seemed happy. No, wait a minute. I remember there was something... a phone call. Yes, she went outside to answer her phone. And when she came back she was very pale and quiet."

Ted Wiley and his nasty phone calls, thinks Hudson.

"Who did Mrs Sutton talk to at the Open Day?" he asks.

"Well, we were standing in a little group and chatting. Margaret Taylor was there...Jennifer, too...and Claire, Claire Hockey."

"Were they good friends of Mrs Sutton?" Hudson asks.

"No, not really. Margaret was the head girl when Penny was 11 years old. Jennifer and Penny were quite good friends. They both slept in the same dormitory and played in the school netball[i] team. Claire was in the same class as Penny but she wasn't really her friend. She hung around with Fiona mostly."

"Do you mean Fiona Lambert?" asks Hudson with interest.

"That's right," Miss Musty sighs. "Fiona was a nightmare!"

"What do you mean?" Hudson asks.

"She was very aggressive and difficult to teach," says Miss Musty.

Hudson writes all of this in his notebook.

"Miss Musty, how long have you lived in Shepton Mallet?"

"Over 30 years, Inspector," she answers.

wheelbarrow	Schubkarre
silk	Seide
to look blank	verständnislos schauen
maiden name	Geburtsname
successful	erfolgreich
nasty	böse
dormitory	Schlafsaal
nightmare	Albtraum

Netball ist ein basketballähnliches Mannschaftsspiel, das im englischsprachigen Raum v.a. Frauen spielen. Netball ist oft Teil des Sportunterrichts.

"So you probably know most of the villagers, then."

She nods.

"Could you look at this, please?"

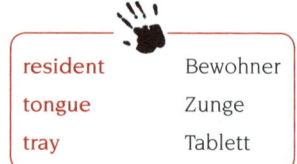

resident	Bewohner
tongue	Zunge
tray	Tablett

Hudson shows her a message that PC Harvey has just sent him. It's a list of the residents of the Sunshine Retirement Home.

"Is there anyone on this list who Penny knew well?"

"Let me see... yes, Miss Sharp. She was headmistress when Penny was a girl. 'Sharp' is the perfect name for her. She has a very sharp tongue. All the girls were frightened of her – so were the teachers!"

Hm... headmistress, thinks Hudson. I wonder if Miss Sharp is the 'HM' in the text message that Penny received.

Exercise 17: Match up the words. Bilden Sie zusammengesetzte Begriffe!

1. ☐ retirement   **a)** person

2. ☐ maiden   **b)** school

3. ☐ public   **c)** name

4. ☐ missing   **d)** home

Jarvis and Cavanagh are sitting on a sofa in a house in Solihull, 10 miles south-east of Birmingham. Mrs Wiley's sister brings them some tea and biscuits on a tray.

"Thanks very much," says Cavanagh happily.

He takes a handful of biscuits and starts to eat. Jarvis gives him a sharp look.

"Mrs Wiley," she says, turning to the small, shy woman sitting opposite her. "Can you tell us where your husband might be?"

Mrs Wiley looks at her nervously but doesn't answer.

Jarvis notices a bruise above her left eye. Poor woman, she's too afraid to talk to us, she thinks.

"We've just been to your house in Dudley, but your husband isn't at home. We need to speak to him quickly. It's about a crime."

Mrs Wiley looks up.

Jarvis goes on, "Penelope Sutton is missing."

Mrs Wiley gasps. "Mrs Sutton!" she whispers.

"She's your lawyer, isn't she?" Jarvis asks gently.

Mrs Wiley nods.

"When did you see her last?" Jarvis asks.

"She came here on Thursday morning. She told me the court has set a date for the trial," replies Mrs Wiley.

"Did you know that your husband was threatening Mrs Sutton on the phone?"

Mrs Wiley just shakes her head sadly.

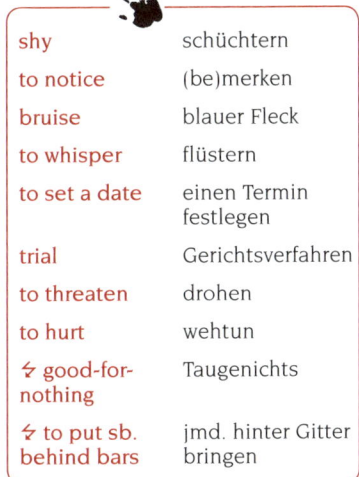

shy	schüchtern
to notice	(be)merken
bruise	blauer Fleck
to whisper	flüstern
to set a date	einen Termin festlegen
trial	Gerichtsverfahren
to threaten	drohen
to hurt	wehtun
⚡ good-for-nothing	Taugenichts
⚡ to put sb. behind bars	jmd. hinter Gitter bringen

"Well, I wouldn't be surprised if Ted has done something to hurt Mrs Sutton," says Mrs Wiley's sister angrily. "He is a good-for-nothing. Look at what he has done to poor Brenda!"

"Lucy, please!" whispers Mrs Wiley.

"Come on, Brenda. Tell the police where that bastard is hiding. It's time he was put behind bars!" She puts her arm round her sister.

"Well, he might be at the **allotment**," says Brenda Wiley in a **shaky** voice. "He sometimes goes there to be alone."

"To **get drunk**, you mean!" says her sister.

"The allotment?" asks Jarvis. Brenda Wiley is silent and looks miserable. She has already said more than she wanted to.

allotment	Schrebergarten
shaky	zitternd
to get drunk	sich betrinken
registration number	Autokennzeichen
ordinary	normal, gewöhnlich
to get on with sb.	mit jmd. auskommen
to bully	mobben, schikanieren
to sleepwalk	schlafwandeln
awful	furchtbar
to bury	begraben

Her sister Lucy answers for her. "I'll give you the address."

"One more thing," says Jarvis. "What kind of car does he drive?"

"A Honda coupé," answers Lucy again. "About two years old, black. Shall I give you the **registration number**?"

Jarvis nods. "Yes, please."

"Tell me more about Fiona Lambert, Miss Musty," says Hudson.

"I heard that she got divorced last year, and that she's looking for a new job. She still lives in the village, you know."

"But this is a boarding school, isn't it? I thought the pupils came from other towns further away."

"Yes, mostly. But we also have some day girls who live locally. They come to school at 9 a.m. and at 3:30 p.m. they go home, just like at an **ordinary** school. Fiona was a day girl."

"Did she come to the open day?"

"I'm not sure. I didn't see her. But there were a lot of people on the lawn, so it's possible that she was there."

"How did she **get on with** Penny?" he asks.

Miss Musty pauses to think before answering. "Fiona and Penny were complete opposites. Penny was very hardworking and polite. I remember Fiona always called her 'Perfect Penny, the teacher's pet'."

"Do you know why Fiona was so angry with Penny?" asks Hudson.

"Yes," Miss Musty sighs. "Penny once told us that she saw Fiona bullying another girl. Fiona got into big trouble for that."

So Fiona hated Penny. So why those text messages? wonders Hudson. He takes Penny's phone out of his pocket and reads:

`1985: A pack of lies!`

Exercise 18: Question words. Lesen Sie weiter und ergänzen Sie die fehlenden Fragewörter!

| what | what | what | who | why |

"Miss Musty, **1.** _____ do you remember about the year 1985?"

Miss Musty puts down her tea cup and rubs her forehead. "1985 was a very sad year for all of us at Shepton Mallet School."

"**2.** _____ ? **3.** _____ happened?" asks Hudson.

"There was a tragic accident. One of our girls was sleepwalking in the upstairs corridor. She fell down the stairs and broke her neck. It was awful! She is buried in the village churchyard."

Hudson sits forward in his chair. "**4.** _____ was she?"

"Her name was Rebecca Bracknell. Poor little Becky."

"**5.** _____ can you tell me about her?" he asks.

"She was a very special child, a **loner** and a day dreamer," she continues. "She wasn't like the other girls, so they **made fun of** her. You know how **cruel** children can be! I remember once a girl put a dead rat in Becky's desk. It nearly **scared her to death**."

"Were you Rebecca's teacher, Miss Musty?"

"I only taught her French. Miss Foster was her class teacher."

"Miss Foster?" Hudson raises his eyebrows.

"Emily Foster. In 1985 she and I were the only young members of **staff**. All the other teachers were at least 50. That seemed old to us back then," she laughs. "Emily and I were good friends. She told me once that she was very worried about Becky. She wanted to put a stop to the bullying, but the girl was too scared to say who it was. When Becky died, Emily was very upset. She didn't want to stay here any longer. She left the school and went to live with some **relatives** in Australia. After that we lost contact, I'm afraid."

loner	Einzelgänger
to make fun of sb.	sich über jmd. lustig machen
cruel	grausam
to scare sb. to death	jmd. zu Tode erschrecken
staff	Personal
relative	Verwandte
curious	neugierig
marble	Marmor
gravestone	Grabstein

"Do you have any idea who was bullying Becky?" asks Hudson.

Miss Musty sighs deeply. "Yes, Penny told us... it was Fiona."

At 5:30 p.m. Hudson is leaving the school when his phone rings.

"Hello, this is Jennifer Blacksmith. Constable Harvey called me and told me to ring this number," says a woman's voice.

Well done again, Harvey, thinks Hudson.

"Thank you for calling, Mrs Blacksmith. I've got a few questions about the school open day last Saturday. You spoke to Penelope Sutton, didn't you? Did you notice anything unusual?"

"No, nothing, Inspector. Is Penny in trouble?"

"I'm afraid she's missing," Hudson replies.

"Oh dear, how terrible!" says Jennifer, shocked.

"Can you think of anything that might help us to find her? Did she say anything strange? Was she worried or scared?"

Jennifer thinks for a moment. "No, we just made small talk really – nothing important," she says. "Then she went outside to take a call. I don't know anything more than that, I'm afraid."

Exercise 19: Choose the correct alternative. Unterstreichen Sie die richtige Variante!

1. Hudson is leaving the school when his phone is ringing / rings .

2. Thank you for call / calling .

3. We both loved / were loving netball when we were at school.

4. I don't know anything more as / than that.

After his talk with Jennifer, Hudson walks back to Fiona's house. I am curious to meet her now, he thinks. But when he arrives at her house there is still no one home. He takes out Penny's phone and rings Fiona's number. No answer!

I must talk to her as soon as possible, but how can I find her?

He decides to take a walk to clear his head. The road from the school leads to the church. He opens a little wooden gate and goes into the churchyard. It is very quiet and peaceful here. He looks around until he finds what he is looking for – a marble gravestone with the words: Rebecca Bracknell 1974 – 1985. There are fresh flowers lying on the grave.

I wonder who put these there? Hudson thinks as he stands looking at the grave. Miss Musty told me that Fiona bullied Rebecca. And Rebecca died. Could there be a connection?

Suddenly he feels a vibration in his pocket. It's Penny's phone. He takes it out and sees that there's a new message:

`51° 11′ 23″ North, 2° 32′ 50″ West.`

Exercise 20: Unscramble the words. Lesen Sie weiter und bringen Sie die Buchstaben in die richtige Reihenfolge!

Those are geographical coordinates, thinks Hudson in

1. sripuser _____. It's from the same

2. munreb _____ as the other **3. xett**

_____ messages. That means it's from Fiona

Lambert. But why would Fiona send Penny a **4. gasseem**

_____ like this?

Hudson opens the GPS function on his own phone and types in the coordinates. It's really close by, he thinks. What's going on? Hudson follows the route along a path to a field behind the church. On one side of the field is a small wood with oak trees. There's no sign of Fiona. Hudson walks to the middle of the field where the coordinates meet.

There he finds a large concrete paving slab with the words "Somerset District Council" carved on it. On top of it someone has left a mobile phone. He picks it up and sees that it is flashing "new message". He opens the message and nearly drops the phone in shock. The message is addressed to himself!

Inspector, long time no kill! Dig deep and solve a crime!

Is someone watching me? thinks Hudson.

He looks around but the field seems to be empty.

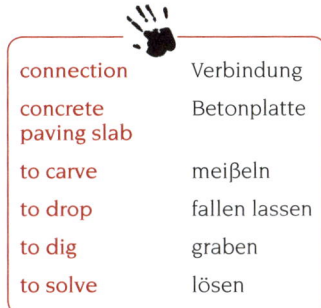

connection	Verbindung
concrete paving slab	Betonplatte
to carve	meißeln
to drop	fallen lassen
to dig	graben
to solve	lösen

Exercise 21: Word spiral. Finden Sie die Begriffe in der Wortspirale!

1	2	3	4	5	6
20	21	22	23	24	7
19	32	33	34	25	8
18	31	36	35	26	9
17	30	29	28	27	10
16	15	14	13	12	11

1-7: an English sport for girls

7-12: the opposite of big

12-20: a critical situation

20-25: a colour

25-30: to think about a question

30-36: the girl that Fiona bullied

Suddenly there is a noise in the little wood at the side of the field. Hudson stares into the woods, but two **magpies** come flying out from between the trees.

Just birds, thinks Hudson and breathes out again. He bends down and examines the paving slab closely. It seems to be a **cover** to something. There are deep **scratches** around the slab. It looks as if someone moved it **by force**.

magpie	Elster
cover	Abdeckung
scratch	Kratzer
by force	mit Gewalt

Time to call the Somerset police, he thinks and dials the number that Harvey gave him earlier.

"Hello, this is Inspector Hudson from Scotland Yard. I need someone to help me move a heavy object."

Caught on Film

"Bradley, tell me what you found out in Basingstoke," says Sir Reginald on Tuesday at 7 p.m. in his office at Scotland Yard.

Bradley proudly holds out the video tape from the CCTV camera. "This film shows the road leading to the scrapyard. I'm sure it will show us who drove the Toyota there last weekend."

"Very good," says Sir Reginald. "So now all you have to do is watch the film carefully, **frame by frame**, for the whole time from Friday evening till Monday morning."

frame by frame	Bild für Bild
⚡ Phew!	Uff!
sleeve	Ärmel

Bradley sighs deeply.

"Yes, that does sound like a lot of work, doesn't it, Bradley? I'm going to give you an assistant to help."

"Thank you, sir!" says Bradley with a grin.

Exercise 22: Fill in the blanks. Lesen Sie weiter und ergänzen Sie die fehlenden Adjektive!

deep   closer   heavy   dark   hard   terrible

"**Phew**, that was **1.**   work!" says young PC Baker from the Warminster police with his **sleeves** rolled up. He and his colleagues are working in the field behind the church in Shepton Mallet, moving the 2. _____ slab that Hudson found. They all wipe the sweat from their foreheads.

"God, what a 3. _____ smell!" Baker says, holding his hand in front of his nose.

The others do the same. Then they step forward to have a 4. _____ look. They see a hole going 5. _____ into the ground.

"It looks like an old well," says Hudson. "It's really 6. _____ down there. I can't see the bottom. Has anyone got a torch?"

PC Stewart comes forward and holds his torch over the well. It looks ghostly in the torchlight.

"Can you see anything?" asks Inspector Matthews.

"No," replies Hudson. "Someone will have to go down there."

"How deep do you think it is?" asks Matthews.

sweat	Schweiß
well	Brunnen
bottom	Boden
torch	Taschenlampe
ghostly	unheimlich

Hudson picks up a stone and throws it into the well. They wait a couple of seconds, then they hear a splash as the pebble hits the water at the bottom of the well.

"It's too deep for us," says Hudson. "This is a job for the police **diving squad**."

I have a very bad feeling about this, he thinks to himself.

In Ashwick, four miles from Shepton Mallet, Dr Willerby looks at his watch. His next patient is very late. He presses the button on his intercom.

diving squad	Polizeitaucher
to cancel	absagen
progress	Fortschritt
anxious	besorgt, ängstlich
armed	bewaffnet
body	*hier*: Leichnam
to cordon off	absperren
council	Gemeinderat
villager	Dorfbewohner

"Mrs Cranmore, has Mrs Lambert **cancelled** her appointment?"

"No, doctor. Maybe she forgot," answers the receptionist.

What a shame, thinks Willerby. We were making good **progress**.

"Jarvis? It's Hudson. Where are you exactly?" Hudson sounds **anxious**.

"Just outside Dudley, sir. Cavanagh and I are on our way to Ted Wiley's allotment. We think he's hiding there."

"Wait where you are. I'm sending a team of **armed** officers to help you," says Hudson in a serious voice. "Be careful, Jarvis. Wiley may be very dangerous. We have just found a **body**. I think it's Penelope Sutton."

Hudson ends the call and looks at his watch. It's 8:30 p.m. He turns to the forensic team, who are working around the well.

"It's getting dark now, so I think we should stop for today. **Cordon off** the area round the well and put a night-watchman on guard." They nod.

"Inspector Matthews, who owns this field?" Hudson asks.

"It belongs to the **council**, Inspector. The **villagers** come here to walk their dogs."

"Right. I'm going to take the body to London for examination. I need Dr Barrington to identify her as soon as possible," says

Hudson. Turning back to the forensic team he continues, "I would like you to go on looking for clues here tomorrow

Bei Adressen steht im Englischen die Hausnummer vor dem Straßennamen.

morning. See if you can find any traces of blood around the well or any signs of a fight. And Inspector Matthews, tell your officers to go door-to-door questioning the villagers. Find out if anyone saw anything suspicious. Please report to me immediately if you find anything."

Why did Fiona lead me here in such a mysterious way? thinks Hudson, puzzled. What does she have to do with Penny's death? It's very important that we find her quickly.

"Constable Baker, you watch Mrs Lambert's house. It's 45 Oaktree Lane. Call me as soon as you see her. I need to talk to her urgently."

Exercise 23: Opposites. Finden Sie die Gegenteile im Text und schreiben Sie sie auf!

1. top _____   4. safe _____

2. early _____   5. life _____

3. funny _____   6. search _____

Meanwhile, in a quiet area just outside Dudley, a team of armed policemen arrive at a group of small allotments. Each one has a small garden hut and a fence around it. It's late on Tuesday evening and the allotments seem to be empty.

"Wiley's is over there," Jarvis whispers, pointing to the middle of the allotment area.

The armed police move slowly and silently towards it. They check that there is no sign of Wiley outside, then they open the gate to his allotment and **creep up to** the hut. Two men with guns stand by the window and another two men guard the door.

"Wiley, are you in there?" shouts an officer.

There's no reply.

"We're coming in!"

puzzled	verblüfft, verwirrt
to creep up to	sich anschleichen an
to catch one's foot	mit dem Fuß hängenbleiben

The men kick the door hard and it flies open. The hut is full of beer bottles and cigarette packets, but Mr Wiley is not there.

"Listen!" says Cavanagh. "I can hear a car!"

They all look through the window and see a black Honda coupé stop next to the allotment gate. A man gets out and walks towards the hut. He is carrying a six-pack of beer.

"Stay where you are and put your hands up!" shouts an officer, running out of the hut and pointing his gun at him.

The man drops his beer in shock and runs as fast as he can. He jumps over the fence into the next allotment.

"Catch him!" shouts Jarvis.

She and Cavanagh jump over the fence and run after him. The next fence is higher. The man tries to jump over it, but it's too high for him and he **catches his foot** on the top. He cries out as he falls face-down on the grass.

"Quick, let's get him!" shouts Jarvis.

> Einige Sammelbegriffe verlangen ein Plural-Verb, wenn man darunter eine Gruppe von Menschen versteht, u.a.
> **police, press, public, staff und team:**
> z.B. *The team are playing well today.*
> or *The staff are unhappy with the changes.*

She and Cavanagh run to where the man is lying. He tries to get up but the two police officers push him down.

Exercise 24: Unscramble the text. Lesen Sie weiter und bringen Sie die Sätze in die richtige Reihenfolge!

a) "Sir, we've got Wiley," says Jarvis on the phone, **out of breath**.

b) "It's him," she says, holding out a bank card with the name Ted Wiley on it.

c) "Good work!" says Hudson. "Bring him to Scotland Yard. I'm on my way back to London, too. We can question him together tomorrow morning."

d) Cavanagh kneels on his back while Jarvis **handcuffs** him and searches his pockets.

1	2	3	4

On Wednesday at 9:30 am, Hudson meets Dr Barrington in his forensic **lab** in London.

"You look tired, Tony," comments Hudson.

"Yes, I am. I worked all night, James. You said it was important to get quick results," replies Barrington.

"Thank you, Tony. So show me what you have found."

The two men walk towards a table. A dead body is lying on the table under a sheet. Hudson **shudders**. This is the part of his job that he really doesn't like. Barrington lifts the sheet.

"As you can see, the body is very **swollen**. She's been in the water for several days. However, I didn't find any water in her lungs, so she was dead before she was put into the well."

"So she didn't **drown**," comments Hudson.

"No, the **cause of death** was this," says Barrington.

He turns the woman's face to one side. On the back of her head Hudson sees a deep cut.

"Someone hit her very hard with a sharp object. Then they threw her body into the well."

"What about the time of death?" asks Hudson.

out of breath	atemlos
to handcuff sb.	jmd. Handschellen anlegen
lab	Labor
to shudder	schaudern
swollen	angeschwollen
to drown	ertrinken
cause of death	Todesursache
sample	Probe
doubt	Zweifel
leather	Leder

"I'd say she died at the weekend, Saturday or Sunday."

"What about the DNA **samples** we gave you? Do they match?"

"Yes, James. The dead woman's DNA matches the blood in the car and the sample we found on Mrs Sutton's toothbrush."

"So there is no **doubt**, Tony. This is Penelope Sutton."

"That's right. But there's something else that I don't understand."

Barrington takes Hudson to the other side of the lab, where Penny's things are lying on a table: her black pencil skirt, white silk blouse, blazer, handbag and a shoe. Barrington picks up the shoe and holds it out to show Hudson.

"This is the wrong size. Mrs Sutton's feet are size 4. This shoe is size 5½ – much too big."

"You mean it's not Mrs Sutton's shoe?" asks Hudson, puzzled.

"Look at it, James. It's very good quality **leather**, but it's been in the water for a very long time, maybe 20 or 30 years."

"Where are Mrs Sutton's shoes, then? Are they still in the well?"

Das Wort **match** wird sowohl als Substantiv als auch als Verb verwendet, mit unterschiedlicher Bedeutung.

match   Streichholz, Partie (beim Sport)

to match   (zusammen)passen

| mood | Laune |

Hudson takes out his phone to call Inspector Matthews in Shepton Mallet. Matthews answers immediately.

"Sir, I was just about to call you," he sounds out of breath. "The divers have found something!"

"A pair of shoes?" asks Hudson.

"Yes! But that's not all. There's another body in the well!"

"What?" Hudson looks at Barrington and then at the old shoe in his hand. "Matthews, send the body and everything else you've found here as soon as possible." And to Dr Barrington he says, "Tony, I'm afraid I've got more work for you."

Exercise 25: Word order. Lesen Sie weiter und bringen Sie die Wörter in die richtige Reihenfolge!

1. Scotland Yard   Hudson   next   back   to   drives

   _____

2. room   he   Jarvis   interview   outside   meets   an

   _____

3. brightly   sir!   says   she   morning

   _____

4. morning   morning?   Wiley   this   Jarvis   Mr   is   how

   _____

"He's is in a very bad **mood** after spending a night in a police cell. He's shouting and swearing[i] at everyone."

56

"Great! Just what I need," says Hudson sarcastically. "I've got a search warrant for Wiley's house in Dudley," Jarvis tells Hudson. "I'm driving back there after we have questioned him."

"Good. But before we go in, I have to make a call. Wait here."

Hudson goes into his office. "Mr Sutton? It's Inspector Hudson from Scotland Yard. I'm afraid I have some very bad news."

"It's Penny, isn't it? Have you found her? Is she okay?" Neil Sutton asks anxiously.

"We have found her. I'm sorry to say..."

"She's dead, isn't she?" Sutton interrupts him. "Oh my God–"

"Mr Sutton, are you still there?" Hudson waits a moment and then continues gently. "Mr Sutton, when could you come to London? I'd like to speak to you **in person**."

Sutton answers in a quiet voice. "I...I'll take the midday train. I can be there in about 3 hours."

"You bloody **pigs** are all the same!" shouts Ted Wiley as Hudson and Jarvis enter the room. "Arresting people for no reason."

Jarvis looks at Hudson. "See what I mean, sir?"

"There I was, **minding my own business**," Wiley continues. "And suddenly my allotment is full of police."

"Mr Wiley, I want to talk to you about Penelope Sutton," says Hudson in a **stern** voice.

Das Verb **to swear** hat zwei Bedeutungen, die man nicht durcheinander bringen sollte! Es heißt „fluchen" aber auch „schwören".

"That bloody bitch! She's ruining me, you know! Brenda met that woman and now she wants a divorce! Well, she can forget it, the stupid cow!"

Hudson bangs his **fist** on the table. "That's enough, Wiley! Mrs Sutton is dead. And you are in big trouble. We know that you threatened her. We found your messages. Now tell me exactly where you were last weekend." Wiley stares at the table. "I won't say a word without my lawyer."

fist	Faust
witness	Zeuge
identity parade	polizeiliche Gegen-überstellung
height	Größe, Höhe
to recognize	wiedererkennen

Just then someone knocks on the door and enters.

"I came as quickly as I could," says the man in a blue suit and a bright red tie. "Bruce Appleton's my name. I'm Mr Wiley's lawyer." He takes a seat next to Ted Wiley.

"So, now that your lawyer is here, let's go on," says Hudson. "Where were you at the weekend, Mr Wiley?"

"I told you already. I was on my allotment, minding my own business." Wiley is still angry, but he is also scared now.

"Any **witnesses**?" asks Jarvis.

"Yeah, my neighbour was there on Saturday morning. And on Sundays the allotments are very busy, so many people saw me."

"What about Saturday afternoon and evening? Did anyone see you there then?" she asks.

"No, but I swear I never touched Mrs Sutton!" Wiley shouts at Jarvis. "God, you women are all the same!"

Jarvis remembers the bruise above Brenda Wiley's eye. "Do you have a problem with women, Mr Wiley?" she asks in a cold voice. "Don't answer that," says Appleton to his client. "You've said enough already."

"Mr Wiley, have you ever been to Shepton Mallet?" asks Hudson. "Shepton what?" replies Wiley. "Never heard of it."

"Well, I've got a witness who saw a man watching the school in Shepton Mallet on Saturday. She is on her way here now," says

Hudson to Appleton. "I'm arranging an identity parade. I'm sure you don't have a problem with that, do you?"
Appleton shakes his head.

Exercise 26: Definitions. Verbinden Sie die Wörter mit ihren Erklärungen!

1. ☐ The police need this to search your house.   a) bruise

2. ☐ A person who sees a crime.   b) lawyer

3. ☐ A blue mark on the skin.   c) witness

4. ☐ You need one if you are in trouble with the police.   d) warrant

---

At 3 p.m. Harvey tells Hudson that Miss Hockey has arrived.
"Thank you for coming here so quickly, Miss Hockey," Hudson says as he takes her into a room with a big window on one wall. "We can see through this window into the next room. But the people on the other side of the glass cannot see us," he explains. "Please take a seat and try to relax. Harvey, send in the men."
Through the window, Claire sees six men standing in a line. The men are all about 40 years old and medium height with dark hair – just like her description of the man with the binoculars. She looks from one face to the next and sighs.
"I'm sorry, Inspector. I don't recognize any of them."
Hudson sighs, too. "Okay, Miss Hockey. That's all for now."
Claire walks along the corridor to the exit. As she is leaving, a man comes in and bumps into her. He doesn't say sorry or even look at her. He just walks on along the corridor, lost in thought.

How **rude**! thinks Claire, watching him go. Wait a minute, I've seen him somewhere before!

Exercise 27: Fill in the blanks. Lesen Sie weiter und vervollständigen Sie die Wörter!

"Please take a **1.** s＿＿＿＿＿＿, Mr Sutton," says Hudson minutes later in his **2.** o＿＿＿＿＿. "Can I get you a coffee or a glass of water?"

Sutton **3.** s＿＿＿＿＿ his head.

Hudson takes a deep **4.** b＿＿＿＿＿ and goes on. "As I said on the phone, we have found your wife. I am very sorry, but it seems she was the victim of a violent **5.** c＿＿＿＿＿."

"Are...are you sure it's Penny?" Mr Sutton asks Hudson.

"Yes, I'm afraid so."

Sutton puts his head in his hands.

"Our forensic expert has tested her DNA. So it's not **necessary** for you to identify her."

"But I want to see her," Sutton says in a quiet voice.

"Of course, Mr Sutton," says Hudson kindly. "I'll drive you to the forensic lab."

On the way to the lab, Mr Sutton is very quiet and lost in thought. Then suddenly he says miserably, "You must find the person who did this terrible thing to my Penny!"

"I will certainly do my best," Hudson answers. "When did you last see your wife?"

"Two weeks ago," Sutton answers. "I came to the house to get some books. And we had a talk."

"What did you talk about?"

"Nothing important. She told me about the school open day."

"I'm sorry, Mr Sutton, but I have to ask you this... I'm sure you understand... Where were you last weekend?" asks Hudson.

"I had a lot of work, so I spent the weekend sitting at my computer in my flat. I'm **renting** it at the moment, just until Penny and I get back together... Oh God, I keep[i] forgetting that she's dead!"

rude	unhöflich
necessary	notwendig
to rent	mieten
to complain	sich beschweren
to escape	fliehen, flüchten
prime suspect	Hauptverdächtiger

"Do you have any witnesses for last weekend, Mr Sutton?"

"No, no one." Mr Sutton puts his hand over his eyes.

"How did it go, sir?" Jarvis asks Hudson an hour later at Scotland Yard.

"It wasn't easy," says Hudson sadly. "Mr Sutton was very upset."

"Hm. Appleton wants to see you, sir," Jarvis says and takes him into the next room.

"Ah, there you are, Inspector," Wiley's lawyer says. "I really must **complain**. You are keeping my client here against his will. And you have no evidence against him."

"It's true that our witness can't identify him. But he threatened Mrs Sutton and he has no alibi for the time of the crime. Plus he tried to **escape** arrest. Wiley is still a **prime suspect**."

Das Verb **to keep** übersetzt man mit „be-/erhalten", aber in Kombination mit einer ing-Form bedeutet es „immer wieder". *I keep forgetting it.* heißt also: Ich vergesse es immer wieder.

"Inspector, you know you can only hold a suspect for a maximum of 96 hours. After that you have to let him go."

Well, I should get moving then, thinks Hudson grimly.

In another room at Scotland Yard, DI Bradley and his assistant are examining the CCTV film from Basingstoke.

"Look, sir!" says young PC Smith excitedly. "I've found something. Saturday evening, 11 p.m."

He and Bradley watch as a Toyota drives past the camera in the direction of the scrapyard.

"Rewind it," says Bradley. "Good, stop right there."

Smith puts the film on pause. Together they stare at the screen.

"Can you magnify it a bit more. Good. Look at that."

They see two people in the car, a driver and a passenger.

Meanwhile Hudson walks down the corridor towards the kitchen. He passes the waiting room and is surprised to see Claire Hockey sitting there. She stands up when she sees him.

"Miss Hockey, why are you still here?"

"I've seen him again! The man with the binoculars," Claire says breathlessly. "He was here. He walked past me."

"Okay, let's go to my office." Hudson leads her to his room where Claire gives him a description of the man.

grimly	grimmig
to rewind	zurückspulen
to magnify	vergrößern
breathlessly	atemlos
neither ... nor	weder ... noch
APB (all points bulletin)	Fahndungs- aufruf
noisy	laut
wallet	Portemonnaie

"Black trousers and a yellow sweatshirt," Hudson repeats slowly. "3:30 p.m., you say, just as you were leaving."

Claire nods. "Yes, exactly."

The man she saw was Mr Sutton, thinks Hudson. What was he doing in Somerset? And why did he lie to us? And what about our other missing witness?

Hudson leaves the room and dials Sutton's number. No answer. He dials Matthews' number again. "Hudson speaking. Have you found Fiona Lambert yet?"

"No, sir. There is no sign of her, **neither** here **nor** in the village."

Hudson goes to the team room. "Harvey, please put out 2 **APBs**: Neil Sutton and Fiona Lambert, our two missing witnesses."

Or suspects? he thinks.

In a **noisy** pub in Birmingham, Neil Sutton sits alone at the bar. "Give me another whisky," he says to the barman.

Just then, Sutton's phone rings. He switches it off. He takes a photo out of his **wallet** and looks at it sadly. Penny, my darling! What went wrong? he sighs, banging his fist on the table.

Exercise 28: Translation. Übersetzen Sie die folgenden Sätze!

1. Ich verbrachte das Wochenende an meinem PC.

_____

2. Sie versucht zu fliehen.

_____

3. Er beschwert sich immer wieder.

_____

4. Ich miete zur Zeit eine kleine Wohnung.

_____

5 The Missing Link

"Come and sit down, James," Miss Paddington tells Hudson on Wednesday evening. "I've made lamb stew for dinner."

"Mmm... it smells delicious!" Hudson smiles as he sits down at the dining table. "It's so good to come home, Miss Paddington, even if it's just for a short break."

"This new case sounds hard. I can't wait to hear about it," says Miss Paddington.

She always enjoys listening to Hudson talk about his work. And she often has some helpful ideas, too. She puts some food on his plate and pours him a glass of wine.

link	Verbindung
to sip	nippen
coincidence	Zufall
thoughtfully	nachdenklich
bloodstain	Blutfleck
track	Spur

James sips his wine and starts to talk. "A woman called Penelope Sutton has been murdered. She was in Somerset for an open day at her old school, Shepton Mallet Boarding School."

"Wait a second, James. Shepton Mallet, you say? I've heard of that school before. Wasn't there a scandal there back in the 80s?"

"Yes, that's right. A pupil fell down the stairs and broke her neck."

"Oh dear. I remember reading about it in the newspaper," says Miss Paddington. "And now an ex-pupil has died at the open day? What a coincidence!"

"I don't really believe in coincidences," Hudson says thoughtfully.

"I know," says Miss Paddington. "That's one reason why you are such a good detective, James."

After dinner, Hudson lies on his bed and closes his eyes. But he can't stop thinking about the case. He picks up Fiona's phone and reads again the text messages she sent to Penny on Saturday:
`1985: A pack of lies!; Ask HM;`
and finally `CU at QA in 10 minutes.`
QA could be the Queen's Arms pub next to the hotel, thinks Hudson. I must go there when I'm back in Shepton Mallet.
He clicks to the strange message Fiona sent him on Tuesday:
`Long time no kill! Dig deep and solve a crime!`
I wish I could solve this crime, he thinks grimly.

Exercise 29: Match-up. Welche der folgenden Begriffe gehören zusammen? Ordnen Sie zu!

1. ☐ sip   **a)** down the stairs
2. ☐ solve   **b)** a drink
3. ☐ fall   **c)** smell
4. ☐ delicious   **d)** a crime

It's 8:30 a.m. on Thursday morning. Hudson is parking his car opposite Tony Barrington's forensic lab when his phone rings. "Good morning! Matthews here. My men have found bloodstains and some interesting tracks leading to the well. We've sent some samples and pictures to forensics, but I'd like to show you in person. Will you be coming back to Shepton Mallet soon?"

"Good work, Matthews. Yes, I'm coming back this afternoon," Hudson replies as he walks towards the lab. "After I've looked at that other body you sent me."

"**Rather you than me**, Inspector!" says Matthews.

Rather you than me!	Lieber Sie als ich!
sight	Anblick
to swallow	schlucken
skull	Schädel
blow	Schlag
asap	schnellstmöglich
mess	Unordnung

"Hello again, James," says Barrington. "We're meeting quite often these days, aren't we?"

"Yes, Tony. Too often," says James, looking at the long table.

Once again there's a body lying under a green plastic sheet.

"Are you ready, James? This is not a pretty **sight**," Barrington says and he pulls back the sheet. On the table is a skeleton.

Hudson **swallows**. "Oh God," he whispers.

"Yes, there's not much left[i] of her, is there? I'd say she's been dead for about 30 years. I can see from the skeleton that this was a young woman – about 25 years old. Her feet are size 5½, just like that old shoe I showed you last time."

"What was the cause of death?" asks Hudson, looking at Barrington so that he doesn't have to look at the body.

"Look at the back of the **skull**," the forensics expert replies. "She died from a **blow** to the head. Just like Mrs Sutton did."

"Do you have any idea who she was?" Hudson asks. "None at all," says Barrington. "But clearly there is a connection between the two dead women."

> **left** hat mehrere Bedeutungen. Als Verb ist es die Vergangenheitsform von **to leave** (verlassen, zurücklassen). Als Adjektiv bedeutet es „links" aber auch „übrig", wie in diesem Fall.

"Yes," Hudson agrees. "And it's my job to find out what it is."

Exercise 30: Correct the mistakes. Lesen Sie weiter und korrigieren Sie die sechs Fehler!

"Listen, everyone. I've got some knew work for you," Hudson tells his team soon afterwards at Scotland Yard. "I want you too check the cases off all missing persons in the Somerset area in the 1980s and 1990s."

"That's a long time ago," comments PC Harvey.

"You're write, Harvey. Long time no kill, just like Fiona Lambert wrote in her message to me. We must find she asap. Where on earth can she be?"

Hudson takes Fiona's phone out of his pocket and hands it to Harvey. "Check all Mrs Lambert's incoming and out-going calls and text messages and let me no if you find anything interesting."

1. _____   4. _____

2. _____   5. _____

3. _____   6. _____

Meanwhile in Dudley, Jarvis and Cavanagh are searching Mr Wiley's house. It's a terrible mess. In the living room they find broken beer bottles all over the floor. Jarvis bends down and picks up a business card from the floor.

"Penelope Sutton, Corbett & Co Lawyers Ltd.," she reads. "It's Mrs Sutton's card. And here's

⚡ So what?!   Ja und?!
sober   nüchtern

the number that Wiley phoned when he made those aggressive calls."

Just then, Cavanagh's phone rings. "Cavanagh here... Hi, Bill... Fine, thanks... Yes... yes... really? Okay, I'll tell her."

He turns to Jarvis. "My colleagues at the station in Birmingham arrested a man for drink-driving last night."

"So what?" says Jarvis impatiently. "We're looking for a murderer. We haven't got time for drink-drivers."

"It's Mr Sutton, Inspector!" Cavanagh explains. "They put him in a cell overnight. He's sober now and ready for questioning."

"Okay. Sorry, Cavanagh," says Jarvis. "We'll go and talk to him as soon as we're finished here. Wiley and Sutton, what a pair! Penny was not very lucky with men, was she?"

An hour later, Jarvis sits down opposite Neil Sutton in an interview room at Birmingham police station. Sutton's hair is a mess and he has dark rings under his eyes.

"Mr Sutton, I'm Inspector Jarvis, a colleague of James Hudson. You spoke to him yesterday, I believe."

Sutton nods.

"Tell me, where were you last Saturday after 4 p.m.?"

"I was at home, working. I already told Inspector Hudson everything I know. Why are you asking me all this again?"

"Mr Sutton, you didn't tell us the truth, did you? We've got a witness who saw you in Shepton Mallet on Saturday afternoon at around 3 o'clock and again that evening at 6:30."

Sutton is silent for a minute. His shoulders are shaking.

"Okay. It's true. I...I was at the school. I was watching Penny."

"You were watching your wife ⓘ?" asks Jarvis. "Why?"

"I thought she was having an affair," says Sutton unhappily. "She told me she was going away for the weekend to visit her old school. But I didn't believe her. I thought she was meeting a man."

"So you followed her there? All the way to Somerset?"

Sutton nods.

"Did your wife see you? Did you speak to her?"

"No. But one of the other guests saw me watching the school. So I drove away quickly. I was back home by 9 p.m."

"Do you have any witnesses for that?" asks Jarvis.

Sutton shakes his head miserably.

"Mr Sutton, you wouldn't be the first jealous husband who killed his wife," Jarvis says sharply.

"Oh God, Penny!" Sutton cries. "I made a terrible mistake!"

Exercise 31: True or false? Welche Aussagen sind korrekt? Markieren Sie mit richtig ✔ oder falsch − !

1. The police have found two dead bodies. ☐
2. Dr Barrington knows who the second dead woman was. ☐
3. DI Jarvis finds the murder weapon in Wiley's house. ☐
4. Mr Sutton lied to the police. ☐

Back at Scotland Yard, DI Bradley points at the computer screen. "Look at this, sir. Here you can see the Toyota as it drives past the factory on the

Woman bedeutet „Frau", wife bedeutet „Ehefrau", z.B. *Please meet my wife*, und nicht *Please meet my woman!*

way to the scrapyard. Smith, pause the film right there... What do you think of that, sir!" says Bradley, proudly.

"Well, I can see two people in the car. But I can't see their faces. Can you magnify it a bit more, Smith?" asks Hudson. "Yes, that's better. Hmm, the passenger is looking at the driver so we can't see his face – just the back of his head. And he is blocking our view of the driver, too. Damn! We can't see the driver's face at all. Just the hands on the steering wheel. But Smith, let's have a close-up of the driver's hands... Now, that's more interesting!"

On the screen they see that the driver's fingernails are painted.

"Our driver is a woman!" says Hudson.

I wonder if it is Fiona Lambert. He calls Inspector Matthews in Shepton Mallet.

"Matthews, Hudson here. Please tell me you've found Lambert."

"Sorry, sir. There's still no sign of her," Matthews replies.

Hudson sighs deeply. Just then there is a knock on the door and WPC Harvey walks in.

"I've checked all the messages on Mrs Lambert's phone," she says. "I'm not sure, but I think this might be important."

She clicks on the voice mail and hands Hudson the phone. He puts it to his ear and listens:

"Hello Mrs Lambert. It's Irene Cranmore, Dr Willerby's receptionist. I'm afraid we will have to change the time of your appointment next week. Please call me back."

"I found Dr Willerby's practice, sir," Harvey says. "It's in Ashwick, about 5 miles from Shepton Mallet. He's a psychologist."

"That means Fiona Lambert had psychological problems. How interesting. I'm going back to Somerset now. I'll visit the doctor as my first priority. Good work, Harvey!" says Hudson.

Exercise 32: Opposites. Lesen Sie weiter und unterstreichen Sie die Gegenteile der angegebene Wörter!

stands up   square   soft   leaves   thin

At 2 p.m. Hudson arrives at Dr Willerby's office in Ashwick. The doctor is sitting in an armchair next to a couch. He watches Hudson carefully through his thick, round glasses as the inspector walks past the couch and chooses a hard wooden chair **instead** and sits down.

"Dr Willerby, I'm trying to contact a patient of yours – Fiona Lambert. I need to talk to her urgently."

Willerby doesn't answer. He just watches Hudson's face.

My God, I'm not here for therapy! thinks Hudson.

At last the doctor replies. "What makes you think that Mrs Lambert is my patient, Inspector?"

"It's very simple. There's a message from your receptionist on her voice mail," answers Hudson smiling.

"Oh... alright, it's true," Willerby says **reluctantly**.

"Why is she coming here?"

"You know I can't tell you that, Inspector." Now Willerby smiles.

Hudson tries again. "Listen, a woman is dead and a murderer is running free. Mrs Lambert is connected to the crime in some way and I have to find her. Do you know where she is?"

"No. All I can say is she missed her appointment on Tuesday and I haven't heard from her since," says the doctor. "Inspector, I've known Fiona Lambert for a very long time. And I have no reason to believe that she would **commit a** violent **crime**."

Exercise 33: Word forms. Ergänzen Sie das jeweilige Substantiv!

1. arrive _____

2. choose _____

3. think _____

4. reply _____

5. die _____

6. connect _____

Shortly afterwards in Shepton Mallet, Hudson walks up the path behind the church on his way to meet Inspector Matthews.

"Excuse me," he says as he walks past a group of villagers who are trying to see what is going on.

"It's no good, son. The police won't let you through," an elderly man tells him.

Hudson sees that Matthews' men have cordoned off a large area around the well, including part of the wood. PC Stewart is on guard, making sure that no one enters the crime scene. He stands back to let Hudson pass.

"Hudson, good to see you," says Inspector Matthews. "Let me show you what we have found."

Matthews leads the way towards the edge of the field near the wood.

"How did the door-to-door questioning go?" Hudson asks as they walk across the field.

"Well, there was a lot going on at the weekend because of the school open day. The village was full of strangers. But no one saw anything suspicious around this field. Now here we are, Hudson. Look at these tracks," he says, pointing at the ground. "Car tyres. And the forensic team found traces of blood here, too. And look here."

Inspector Matthews points at another track going across the field to the well. "As you can see, it's from just one wheel. But it's too wide for a bicycle."

"You're right, Matthews. I wonder what made this track."

"Excuse me, sir," says young PC Baker. "I really like gardening. I've got some lovely roses in my garden."

"Baker, get back to work. Can't you see we're busy?" Matthews says angrily.

"But, sir! This track is just like the mark that my wheelbarrow makes in the mud."

"He's right, you know," says Hudson. "A wheelbarrow. There must be lots of them in this village. Matthews, you'll have to send

| elderly | älterer |
| edge | Rand, Kante |

your men round the village again. Tell them to make a list of everyone who owns a wheelbarrow. And find out if someone's wheelbarrow is missing."

Hudson walks a few steps towards the churchyard and takes Fiona's phone out of his pocket. He reads her message again:

Dig deep and solve a crime!

Why did Fiona lead me here? Hudson asks himself. And why did she send me this strange message? Why didn't she contact me directly? What does she have to do with Penny's death? And who is the other dead woman? So many questions but no answers! The link between Penny and Fiona lies far in the past. Perhaps I need to dig deeper into the past to find a clue, he thinks.

He has an idea. He gets in his car and drives off to the Sunshine Retirement Home on the other side of the village.

So this is the woman who was so strict that all the pupils and teachers were scared of her, Hudson thinks.

"May I speak to you, Miss Sharp?" he asks politely.

"Pssst," she replies. "Be quiet. I'm missing my programme."

"Miss Sharp, I'm Inspector Hudson from Scotland Yard."

But she ignores him, so Hudson walks over to the radio and turns it off. Miss Sharp looks up angrily.

"I'm here on important police business," Hudson continues.

"Alright, young man. Tell me what this is about," she says in a voice that makes Hudson feel like a schoolboy again.

"Yes, Miss Sharp. A **former** pupil of Shepton Mallet School has been murdered – Mrs Penelope Sutton. Maybe you remember her as Penny Braithwaite."

Miss Sharp frowns as she tries to remember. "Ah, Penny, a

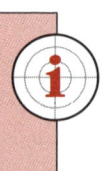

Die British Broadcasting Corporation, kurz **BBC**, ist eine britische Rundfunkanstalt, die mehrere Hörfunk- und Fernsehprogramme betreibt.

good girl, very polite. Someone murdered her, you say. How terrible!"

"Last Saturday she phoned the retirement home. I think she wanted to talk to you. Do you have any idea what she wanted?"

rocking chair	Schaukelstuhl
former	ehemalig
to reach for sth.	nach etw. greifen
to come to no good	böse enden

"Penny wanted to see me? That's unusual! Not many of my ex-pupils or staff have been to visit me, you know."

I'm not surprised, thinks Hudson.

"So you don't know what it was about?" he asks again.

Miss Sharp shakes her head and reaches for her radio.

Exercise 35: Synonyms. Finden Sie die Synonyme im Text und schreiben Sie sie auf!

1. frightened   _____

2. significant   _____

3. strange   _____

4. go on   _____

"Wait, Miss Sharp. There's something else," Hudson says. "I need to find another ex-pupil – Fiona Lambert. What can you tell me about her?"

Miss Sharp sighs. "I always knew Fiona would come to no good!"

"What do you mean?"

Miss Sharp closes her eyes for a moment to think. "Fiona was a rebel. Of course, she had a difficult home life, which is probably why she was so much trouble..."

She pauses, lost in thought. "I remember it all quite clearly. Fiona's father was dead. Fiona's mother wanted her to go to Shepton Mallet School, but it's quite expensive, you know. The poor woman was always working, trying to **earn** the money to pay the **school fees**. "

"How did Fiona get on at Shepton Mallet School?" Hudson asks.

"It was difficult for her," Miss Sharp tells him. "She felt quite bitter about the other girls, because most of them came from rich families. But she wasn't stupid. Her **grades** were quite good... to begin with. Then suddenly, around the end of 1985, they started to get worse and worse.[i] And after that she was a nightmare for the teachers. They couldn't control her at all. In the end I decided to speak to her mother. I told her that maybe Fiona would be happier at the local **comprehensive school**. So in 1986 she left."

"And what about Fiona's **relationship** to Penny?" Hudson asks.

"Well, the class teacher Emily Foster was very worried about one of the girls in the same class as Fiona and Penny, because someone was bullying her. Miss Foster told me she wanted to find out who the bully was. But no one would tell her – no one except Penny. She was braver than the others. She told her teacher that it was Fiona. After that Fiona hated Penny."

"Was Fiona ever **physically** aggressive towards Penny?"

to earn	verdienen
school fees *pl*	Schulgebühren
grades *pl*	*hier*: Noten
comprehensive school	Gesamtschule
relationship	Beziehung
physically	körperlich
letter of resignation	Kündigungsbrief
manners *pl*	Benehmen

worse and worse bedeutet „immer schlimmer". Diese Struktur kann man mit allen Adjektiven verwenden, z.B. *She understood more and more.* Sie verstand immer mehr.

Miss Sharp thinks hard about this. "I can't remember. The class teacher would know more about that than I do."

"Miss Foster?" asks Hudson. "How can I contact her?"

Miss Sharp looks very angry. "I don't know and I don't want to know! She suddenly left the school back in 1985, but she didn't even tell me she was going! She just wrote a **letter of resignation** and left in the middle of the night – went to live on her brother's farm in Australia. No respect! No **manners**!"

"Did she leave a contact address in her letter?" asks Hudson.

Miss Sharp frowns again. "You are asking a lot of difficult questions, young man. I'm 86, you know! I can't remember everything. Why don't you read the letter yourself? It should still be in the school archives somewhere."

"Yes, I'll do that. Thank you very much for your time, Miss Sharp." Hudson gets into his car and drives straight to Shepton Mallet School.

So what is the evidence so far? he thinks as he drives along. Fiona has psychological problems. As a child she hated Penny. Now Penny is dead and Fiona has disappeared. All the evidence points towards Fiona. But how can I find her? And why do I have the feeling that Miss Foster may be the missing link?

 **Lost Friends**

At 5 p.m. Hudson walks up the path towards Shepton Mallet School once again. It's very quiet and there is no one in sight. He rings the doorbell. A minute later Miss Musty opens the door.

"Ah, Inspector," she says with a warm smile. "Do come in."

"Thank you, Miss Musty. I'd like to ask you some more questions."

"Of course. Come this way," she says and she leads him along the corridor and up the stairs to her office on the first floor.

Exercise 36: Choose the correct alternative. Lesen Sie weiter und unterstreichen Sie die richtige Variante!

"It's very **1.** quiet / quite here today," comments Hudson as he takes a seat.

"Yes, the summer holidays have started. There's only me and my secretary **2.** hear / here now, finishing **3.** some / any paper work."

"Miss Musty, you told **4.** my / me before about Miss Foster who worked here in the 1980s. Have you got her address or phone number?"

"No, I'm afraid not," she says **5.** sad / sadly . "We lost touch when she left. We haven't spoken since 1985."

"I see. Please tell me about your time working together."

Miss Musty pauses to think. "Emily and I were good friends. She was like a sister to me. We were about the same size, you know. So we often borrowed [i] each other's clothes and shoes!"

"If you were such good friends, why did you lose touch? Didn't you ever try to contact her at her brother's farm in Australia?"

Miss Musty looks puzzled. "Her brother's farm? But Emily hasn't got a brother! She's an only child."

"Did she tell you that?" asks Hudson.

"Yes, she said her parents are already dead. The only other relatives she has are some cousins who live in Brisbane."

"Miss Sharp told me that when Emily went she left a letter behind. Have you read it, Miss Musty?"

"No, I haven't. It was addressed to Miss Sharp, not to me," she replies. "Emily didn't leave any message at all for me."

"I would like to look at the letter," Hudson continues. "Miss Sharp said it must be in the archives. Can you find it for me?"

Miss Musty stands up and walks past a shelf of sports trophies. Then she opens a door to a small room full of filing cabinets.

"Oh dear, I have no idea where the records for 1985 are. Mrs Motherwell would know, but she has left work already today."

Borrow und lend bedeuten beide „leihen, ausleihen". Aber Vorsicht! Borrow benutzt man, wenn man sich etwas ausleiht. Lend verwendet man, wenn man etwas verleiht. z.B.
*Can I borrow your car? = Can **you** lend **me** your car?*

"I'll help you," says Hudson. And together they search through the files.

"Inspector, I think I've found it," Miss Musty says fifteen minutes later and hands Hudson an old brown envelope with Miss Sharp's name on it.

79

Hudson opens the old envelope and pulls out a piece of paper.

I have decided to give up teaching and go to help my brother on his farm in Brisbane.

"It's signed 'Emily Foster', but she doesn't give her brother's address."

"Brother? I don't understand!" Miss Musty says, surprised.

There's something strange about this letter, thinks Hudson. I think I have seen that writing before. How can that be?

"Thank you, Miss Musty. I'd like to take this with me," he says and puts the letter in his pocket.

As soon as he is outside the school he calls Harvey. "Hudson here. I want you to find a farm in the Brisbane area of Australia. The farmer's name is Foster."

Exercise 37: Where does it happen? Verbinden Sie die Ereignisse mit den Orten.

1. ☐ The teenagers crash the car in ...

   a) Birmingham.

2. ☐ Penny worked at a law company in ...

   b) Shepton Mallet.

3. ☐ Hudson is staying at the White Hart Hotel in ...

   c) Dudley.

4. ☐ The police arrest Mr Wiley on his allotment in ...

   d) Brixton.

An hour later, Hudson and Miss Musty meet again, this time at the police station in Warminster.

"Inspector Hudson, I really must complain! Why have you brought Henry here? What has he done?" Her cheeks are red with anger.

"It's always the same," says Mrs Motherwell, who is standing next to her with tears in her eyes. "People don't understand Henry. They are afraid of him because he's handicapped. But I swear he wouldn't hurt a fly."

So that's why he won't answer any of my questions, thinks Hudson. He looks at Henry, who is sitting at a table and staring out the window in silence.

"Come with me, please, and I'll explain," Hudson says, and he leads the two women into another room.

"One of our officers tried to question Henry at his cottage. But when Constable Baker asked to see his wheelbarrow, Henry ran inside and locked the door. Do you have any idea why?"

cheek	Wange
handicapped	behindert
He wouldn't hurt a fly.	Er kann keiner Fliege etwas zuleide tun.
cottage	Häuschen, kleines Landhaus
shed	Schuppen
in tears	in Tränen aufgelöst
to promise	versprechen

Both women look puzzled and shake their heads.

"I'd like to see that wheelbarrow. Can you tell me where it is?"

"It's in the school's garden shed. I'll show you," Miss Musty says.

"How long are you going to keep my brother here?" asks Mrs Motherwell in tears.

"No longer than necessary, I promise," answers Hudson.

"Baker, can you call the police psychologist? Tell him I need him to help me question a witness. Ask him to meet me here in an hour," Hudson says as he leaves the station with the two women.

Exercise 38: Translation. Lesen Sie weiter und fügen Sie die richtige Übersetzung ein!

It's 8 p.m. when Hudson parks the car at the [1. Rand] _____ of the field [2. hinter] _____ the church in Shepton Mallet. He and one of his passengers [3. aussteigen] _____ of the car.

"Thank you for coming, Dr Willerby," says Hudson. "Our police psychologist is [4. beschäftigt] _____ and I don't [5. warten wollen] _____ any longer."

"I'm happy to help, Inspector," replies the doctor. "So you think the killer used a wheelbarrow to move the body."

"Yes, I think he did. Look, here are the tracks."

"You said "he". Are you sure it was a man?" asks Willerby.

"Probably. Whoever put the body in the well was strong enough to move the heavy concrete cover," Hudson replies. "I went to the school to examine Henry's wheelbarrow, but it has disappeared. I think he knows something about this and I want to know what."

Hudson opens the car door to let the other passenger out.

"Come with me, Henry," Dr Willerby says. "We want to show you something."

He holds Henry's arm and leads him across the field towards the well. As they come closer to the well, Henry gets very nervous. He tries to pull his arm away, but the doctor holds on tight.

"Don't worry, Henry. No one is going to hurt you," he says calmly.

"Did you come here last Saturday night, Henry?" Hudson asks.

Henry tries **desperately** to get away.

"That's enough for today, Inspector," says Dr Willerby **firmly**. "He's clearly frightened and he doesn't understand what's going on. I think you should let him go home now."

"Okay," Hudson agrees reluctantly. "But we must try to talk to him again tomorrow."

to hold on tight	fest halten
desperately	verzweifelt
firmly	fest
headache	Kopfweh
tiled	gefliest
shape	Form
to get rid of	loswerden

Exercise 39: Unscramble the adjectives. Bringen Sie die Buchstaben in die richtige Reihenfolge!

1. mrif _____

3. rgtnso _____

2. sovreun _____

4. httgi _____

Fiona wakes up with a terrible **headache**. She's lying face down on a cold **tiled** floor. She tries to move, but her hands and feet are tied tightly.

Where am I? she thinks in panic.

She rolls onto her back and tries to focus her eyes. It's very dark except for the moonlight shining through a window. She sees the **shapes** of two people, but she can't see their faces.

"What are we going to do now?" whispers one of them. "There are police all over the village! We have **to get rid of** her quickly. We can't leave her here any longer. Come on, help me move her."

On Friday morning in the hotel breakfast room, Hudson is looking at Penny's phone and thinking. 'CU at QA in 10 minutes'...

Did Fiona mean the Queen's Arms? I should go there straight away.

underage	minderjährig
landlord	*hier*: Wirt
to be deep in conversation	ins Gespräch vertieft sein
The time is up.	Die Zeit ist abgelaufen.
to insist	auf etw. bestehen

He finishes his breakfast quickly and walks to the pub next door. The Queen's Arms doesn't open until 11 a.m., but a bald man with a beer belly is already cleaning the tables in the beer garden.

"Morning, I'm Inspector Hudson from Scotland Yard."

The man looks up in surprise. "Is this about those **underage** drinkers[i] at the weekend?" he asks nervously.

"No, it isn't," says Hudson. "Can we go inside to talk?"

"Yes, of course. My name's Lewis. I'm the **landlord** here," he says and he leads the way into the pretty little black and white building.

The two men sit at the bar.

"Would you like a beer?" Lewis asks.

"No thanks, I never drink on duty," Hudson replies. "Mr Lewis, I'd like to ask you some questions. Did you see this woman in the pub on Saturday evening?" He holds out a photo of Penny Sutton.

Lewis looks at it carefully. "Yes, I remember her. A pretty woman."

"Right," says Hudson. "Was she here alone?"

"No, they were sitting over there in the corner." He points to a table on the other side of the room."

In Großbritannien ist der Verkauf und Konsum von Alkohol in der Öffentlichkeit für alle unter 18 Jahren verboten.
Jedoch darf man ab 16 in Restaurants und Bars Bier, Wein oder Cider (Apfelwein) zu einer Mahlzeit trinken, wenn eine Person über 18 Jahren die Bestellung aufgibt.

"They?" asks Hudson.

"Yeah, the woman in the photo and Fiona from Oaktree Lane."

"Did you notice anything unusual. Did they have an argument?"

"No, they **were deep in conversation** for a while. And then they got up and left together."

"What time was that?" asks Hudson.

"About 10 p.m.," says Lewis. "I haven't seen either of them since."

Exercise 40: Mixed verb forms. Lesen Sie weiter und setzen Sie die Verben in der richtigen Form ein!

be	have	leave	miss	ring	think

Hudson is just **1.** _____ the pub when his phone **2.** _____ .

"This **3.** _____ Jarvis speaking. We **4.** _____ a problem. Ted Wiley is **5.** _____ ."

"Wiley? I **6.** _____ he was safe in our police cell."

"We had to let him go yesterday evening, sir," Jarvis explains. "**The time was up** and Appleton **insisted**."

"Damn lawyers!" says Hudson angrily. "So where is Wiley now?"

"We don't know. Lucy Johnson called the police station last night."

"That's Brenda Wiley's sister, right?" asks Hudson.

"Yes, sir. She said Wiley was banging on the door of her house and swearing. But when our officers arrived, he was gone. We've checked his house and his allotment, but he's disappeared."

"So one of our prime suspects is running free," Hudson says.

"I'm afraid so, sir," Jarvis replies miserably.

Just then Hudson's phone beeps as a text message arrives from Harvey at Scotland Yard:

I've got news! Please call me back.

"Jarvis, I've got to make another call. I'll speak to you later." Hudson calls Harvey.

"Inspector, I've found out something!" Harvey sounds excited. "I tried to trace Miss Foster in Brisbane, but there was no sign of her or her brother and his farm."

| habit | Gewohnheit |

"Is that your news?" asks Hudson, disappointed.

"No, sir. There's more. What I *did* find were Miss Foster's cousins. They live on the coast in a little town called Castaway Beach, south of Brisbane. I spoke to them, and guess what? They told me that their cousin Emily doesn't have any brothers or sisters. And they haven't heard from her for 30 years!"

"It sounds as if Miss Foster never went to Australia," says Hudson thoughtfully. "Thank you, Harvey. That's very interesting."

Next he dials the number of the forensic lab in London.

"Tony, Hudson here. Can you to send me a photo of a piece of evidence?"

It's 10 o'clock and Hudson is sitting in Miss Musty's office again. "This is becoming a **habit**, Inspector," Miss Musty says. "Mrs Motherwell, could you bring us some tea, please?"

The secretary nods and walks off towards the kitchen.

"Is this about Henry?" she asks after Mrs Motherwell has left.

"No, Miss Musty. I want to talk to you about your old friend, Miss Foster. You told me that you were very close, almost like sisters."

"Yes, we were," she replies sadly. "I missed her when she left."

"You told me you shared each other's clothes," Hudson continues. "Do you recognize this shoe?"

Hudson holds out his phone. On it he has several photos of the shoe that the divers found in the well.

Miss Musty looks at them carefully for some time.

Then she whispers, "That's my shoe!"

Hudson's phone rings. Damn! he thinks.

"Excuse me just a moment, Miss Musty," he says and goes outside to take the call.

"Matthews here. Inspector, I've got Dr Willerby with me. We're at the cottage to pick up Henry for questioning. But he's gone."

"Okay, tell your men to search the area and find him. I'm in the middle of something important. I'll be there later."

He rings off [i] and goes back into Miss Musty's room.

"Where did you find my shoe?" she whispers in shock.

"Miss Musty, as you know we are investigating a murder."

"Yes, I know. Poor Penny," she replies.

"We found this shoe at the crime scene. It was at the bottom of a well," Hudson tells her and watches her face carefully.

Miss Musty frowns. "How did it get there? I don't understand."

"When did you last see this shoe?" he asks.

"In 1985. Emily wanted to go to a party in Warminster," Miss Musty remembers. "She borrowed my best shoes. That was about two weeks before she went to Australia. She forgot to give them back to me when she left. I was quite angry about that."

"We have been trying to find Miss Foster in Brisbane. It seems she never went to Australia at all," Hudson says gently.

"Well, where is she then?" Miss Musty is confused and upset.

Phrasal Verbs
Das Verb **to ring** wird mit verschiedenen Präpositionen verwendet:
to ring sb. up jmd. anrufen
to ring back zurückrufen
to ring off den Hörer auflegen

"I'm sorry to have to tell you this," says Hudson quietly. "We found a second body at the crime scene, together with your shoe. It seems there was another murder... about 30 years ago."

Miss Musty looks at him open-mouthed. Then she covers her face with her hands and starts to cry.

Exercise 41: Match-up. Verbinden Sie die Begriffe!

1. ☐ prime   a) evidence
2. ☐ close   b) suspect
3. ☐ piece of   c) scene
4. ☐ crime   d) friend

Just then Mrs Motherwell walks in and puts the tea tray on the table. She gives Hudson a cold look and leaves the room.

Hudson pours the tea and hands a cup to Miss Musty.

"I think you are hiding something," says Hudson sternly. "If you and Emily were so close, why didn't you stay in contact? Didn't you think it was strange that you never heard from her again? Why don't you tell me the whole truth?"

Miss Musty sighs. "Emily and I had a bad argument... about what happened to Becky."

She closes her eyes for a moment to remember. "I can see it all clearly, as if it were yesterday. It's 1985. I'm coming back to the school after an evening out with Larry, my boyfriend. We've been to the cinema in Ashwick to see 'Back to the Future'. I say good-bye to Larry outside the school gate and then I start walking up the path. Suddenly I see Henry. He comes running out of the school. He seems frightened and he runs home to his cottage. I think, how strange. What has he been doing in the school at this time of night? And I'm surprised to see that all the lights are on in

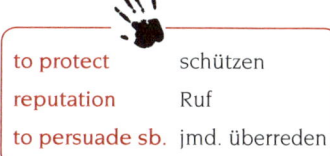

to protect	schützen
reputation	Ruf
to persuade sb.	jmd. überreden

the entrance hall. Everyone usually goes to bed early in a boarding school, Inspector." She pauses.

"What happened next?" Hudson says gently.

"I open the front door and go in. There's a group of teachers and girls standing at the bottom of the stairs. And someone is lying on the floor covered with a sheet. Emily is talking to the police on the telephone. She was always good in an emergency. She says, 'Come quickly! One of our girls has fallen down the stairs. I'm afraid she is dead!'"

"Was it Rebecca Bracknell?" asks Hudson.

She nods.

"Do you think Henry had something to do with Rebecca's death?"

"No," she replies. "He's completely harmless. But I thought it was strange how he reacted, so I decided to tell Miss Sharp."

Hudson nods. He remembers Fiona's text messages: '1985: A pack of lies' and 'Ask HM'.

"Please go on, Miss Musty."

"So I go to see Miss Sharp. I'm a bit scared of her, but I tell her about Henry and ask her if we should tell the police."

"What did she say to that?" Hudson asks.

"She said, 'No, we don't need to talk to the police again. You know that Henry is harmless. Rebecca's death was a terrible accident. We don't want even more scandal about the school.'"

"So she wanted to **protect** the school's **reputation**," says Hudson. "Did you agree to that?"

"Well, I wasn't sure about it at first. It didn't seem right, not telling the police. But she **persuaded me**."

"How did she do that?" Hudson asks with interest.

"I remember she said that I was doing a great job and she offered me the post of **deputy** headmistress."

"So you kept your mouth shut and she gave you a promotion."

deputy — Stellvertreter

Exercise 42: Translation quiz. Übersetzen Sie die Begriffe und finden Sie das Lösungswort!

1. Tablett   _ _ □ _

2. Wahrheit   _ _ □ _ _

3. überreden   _ _ _ □ _ _ _ _

4. Unfall   _ _ _ _ _ _ □

5. Ruf   □ _ _ _ _ □ _ _ _

6. harmlos   _ _ _ _ □ _ _

7. Lügner   _ □ □ _

Lösung: □ □ □ □ □ □ □ □ □

The Sports Trophy

Fiona **is blindfolded** now and her arms are still tied behind her back. She tries to move her hands but her fingers just **scratch** the floor underneath her. She gives a little scream

to be blindfolded	die Augen verbunden haben
to scratch	kratzen
splinter	Splitter
gagged	geknebelt

when a **splinter** goes under her nail. The floor is no longer tiled. It feels like wood.

Where am I now? What's going on? She tries to shout for help but her mouth is still **gagged**.

Exercise 43: Unscramble the words. Lesen Sie weiter und bringen Sie die Buchstaben in die richtige Reihenfolge!

"You **1. dlot** _____ me that you and Miss Foster had an **2. matgeunr** _____ about Becky," Hudson asks Miss Musty. "Tell me more **3. utboa** _____ that."

"It was shortly after Becky **4. eidd** _____," Miss Musty says. "Emily seemed **5. tuspe** _____.

She told me that on the evening of the accident, from her bedroom window she saw Henry running across the garden. She thought she should tell the police."

"And what did you say to her?" Hudson asks.

"I said, 'No, don't do that! Think

tap	Wasserhahn
hosepipe	Wasserschlauch
attached	befestigt
⚡ to get somewhere	vorankommen (mit etw.)
handle	Griff
to fetch	herbeiholen
to pull oneself together	sich zusammen-reißen

of the scandal!' Then I told her to talk to Miss Sharp about it," replies Miss Musty. "That's when Emily got really angry with me. 'All you care about is your career,' she shouted. But she did what I asked. She went to see Miss Sharp... And I never saw her again." Hudson's phone rings.

"Hudson, it's me again," says Inspector Matthews.

"Have you found Henry yet?" Hudson asks.

"No, but we've found the wheelbarrow. Stewart found it at the school. The forensic team are checking it right now. I'm here with them. It looks as if someone washed it recently."

"Someone who has something to hide. Where exactly are you?"

"Just outside the back of the school building," Matthews replies.

"I'm in the headmistress's office. I'll come and meet you in two minutes." Hudson turns back to Miss Musty who is looking very pale. "I'm afraid you were wrong about Henry," he tells her. "We must find him as soon as possible."

"This is where I found it, sir," PC Stewart says minutes later.

He points to a wheelbarrow which is standing in front of a door in a wall. Hudson sees a **tap** on the wall, with a garden **hosepipe attached** to it. They walk over to the forensic officers who are busy examining the wheelbarrow.

"We think someone used that hosepipe to clean it," Stewart says.

"So we won't find much then," says Hudson, disappointed.

"I wouldn't say that, sir," answers a young woman in white overalls. "Look here. They forgot to wash the bottom. This looks like a bloodstain to me. By the way, my name's Nancy."

"Good work, Nancy! Now we're finally getting somewhere."

Behind the wheelbarrow there is a wooden door. Hudson tries to turn the handle but the door is locked.

"I'll fetch the keys," he says and walks back inside to Miss Musty's office.

She is still sitting at her desk looking very pale.

"Miss Musty, I know this is a shock for you, but I think a criminal is hiding somewhere in the school and I need your help. Please give me the keys for the building."

Miss Musty pulls herself together. "Yes, of course, Inspector. Mrs Motherwell has them in her desk."

They walk to the secretary's office next door. The room is empty.

"She's left already. Never mind, I know where she keeps them."

Exercise 44: Translation. Übersetzen Sie die Sätze!

1. By the way, my name's Nancy.

   _____

2. Pull yourself together!

   _____

3. Now we're finally getting somewhere.

   _____

4. I'll fetch the keys.

   _____

Miss Musty opens a drawer and hands Hudson a heavy **key ring**.

| key ring | Schlüsselbund |

"Come with me and show me which key fits which door."

Minutes later Hudson unlocks the door behind the wheelbarrow. It opens onto a dark corridor. Near the end of the corridor there is another door.

"This leads to the girls' shower room," Miss Musty explains. "How strange! The shower room key is missing."

"Henry! Are you in there?" Hudson shouts and he bangs his fist on the locked door.

There is no answer.

"Baker, Stewart. Help me open this door."

The two young officers run at the door and hit it with their shoulders. It moves a little but doesn't open. They run at it again. This time there is a loud bang and the door flies open.

"Look at that!" Baker says, rubbing his shoulder.

In one corner the white floor tiles are covered in blood.

"Get the forensic team in here," Hudson says.

Seconds later Nancy appears.

"Inspector Hudson, we've found some more blood outside," she says. "And a track going across the garden."

"Show me," Hudson orders. "And ask your team to examine this room. I want to know if Fiona Lambert has been here."

Outside Nancy points to some marks in the wet grass. They lead from the school, across the garden and into a field behind it.

"What's over there?" Hudson asks Miss Musty.

"That's the school sports ground," she replies.

"Okay, men, come with me. You too, Miss Musty. I may need your help again. Matthews, where is Dr Willerby now?"

"He's waiting in the car over there," Matthews points to a police car in the school car park.

"Good, bring him along, too. He may be useful."

Exercise 45: Prepositions. Lesen Sie weiter und unterstreichen Sie alle sechs Präpositionen!

Together they follow the track past the tennis courts[i] and towards the hockey pitch.[i] Next to it Hudson sees a small wooden building.

"The girls keep their tennis rackets and hockey sticks in there," Miss Musty explains.

"Is there another way in, besides that door?" Hudson asks.

"No, Inspector, but there's a large window at the back."

"Baker, Stewart, cover the back window. Matthews, you and I will try the front door. Miss Musty, Dr Willerby, please wait here."
Hudson and his men move carefully towards the building.
"Henry, are you there?" shouts Hudson as he walks forward.
"Stay where you are!" a woman's voice shouts back. "Leave us alone or Fiona dies!"

"Oh my God, that's Mrs Motherwell!" Miss Musty exclaims as she recognizes her secretary's voice.

"Yes, and she's got Fiona – just as I thought," says Hudson.

He and Matthews stand still. "I just want to talk to you, Mrs Motherwell," Hudson says in a calming voice. "You are only making the situation worse for yourself... and for Henry."

Der Begriff „Platz, Spielfeld" wird verschieden übersetzt, je nachdem welche Sportart gemeint ist:	
tennis **court**	Tennisplatz
football **pitch**	Fußballplatz
golf **course**	Golfplatz
So ähnlich ist es auch bei Schlägern:	
tennis **racket**	Tennisschläger
hockey **stick**	Hockeyschläger
golf **club**	Golfschläger

"Don't talk to me about Henry!" she screams hysterically. "I've spent my whole life trying to protect him from people like you – people who don't understand what a lovely, gentle person he is."

equipment	Ausrüstung
throat	Hals
to collapse	zusammen-brechen
relieved	erleichtert
wicked	böse
responsible	verantwortlich

Hudson slowly takes another step forward. Through the window at the front of the shed he sees a room full of sports **equipment**. Mrs Motherwell is standing in the middle with her arm around Fiona's neck. She is holding a knife to her **throat**.

"Please don't do anything stupid, Mrs Motherwell. Put the knife down and let's talk about this."

"There's nothing to talk about. This has all gone too far. I've done my best for Henry, but it's no good..."

A crash of broken glass interrupts Mrs Motherwell. She turns round in surprise and sees Baker pointing a gun at her through the back window.

"Put your hands up!" he shouts.

Mrs Motherwell screams and drops her knife to the ground.

"Quick, Matthews," says Hudson.

Together they run in and grab Mrs Motherwell from behind, holding her arms tightly.

"Miss Musty, call an ambulance," Hudson shouts over his shoulder as Fiona **collapses** on the floor.

"Dr Willerby, come quickly!"

The doctor runs into the shed and kneels on the floor next to his patient.

In the corner of the room, Henry stands watching in silence as the policemen put handcuffs on his sister. He looks strangely relaxed... even **relieved**.

Exercise 46: Find the opposites. Finden Sie die Gegenteile im Text und schreiben Sie sie auf!

1. calmly   _____
2. intelligent   _____
3. aggressive   _____
4. intact   _____
5. loosely   _____

"Where's Henry?" Mrs Motherwell asks as Hudson and Matthews sit down opposite her in the Warminster police station. Her voice is shaky and her eyes are red from crying.

"He's alright," Hudson replies. "Dr Willerby is taking care of him. Mrs Motherwell, we've got a lot of questions for you. Let's start with Fiona Lambert. Why did you kidnap her?"

"I just wanted to frighten her so she wouldn't go to the police. It worked before."

"What do you mean, 'It worked before'?" asks Matthews.

"Back in 1985...," she bites her fingernails for a moment. "Fiona was a wicked girl, you know. She was responsible for Rebecca's death. That's what I told her when she came to see me... when she told me that terrible story..."

"I've read about the case," Matthews interrupts. "The police said it was an accident. How can Fiona be responsible?"

"Fiona bullied Rebecca. The poor girl was traumatized. That's why she started sleepwalking. That's why I told Fiona she was a murderer!" Mrs Motherwell's voice is louder now and there is a wild look in her eyes.

Now Hudson interrupts. "What terrible story did Fiona tell you?"

"One afternoon she came to see me. She was very frightened. This is what she told me." Mrs Motherwell takes a deep breath and suddenly she is back in the past. "It's a dark, rainy evening and Fiona is hiding in the wood behind the

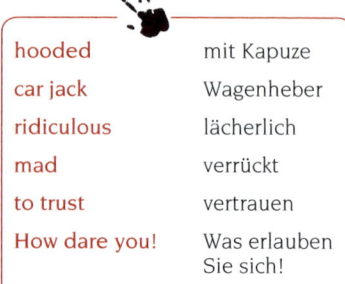

hooded	mit Kapuze
car jack	Wagenheber
ridiculous	lächerlich
mad	verrückt
to trust	vertrauen
How dare you!	Was erlauben Sie sich!

church. She often goes there to smoke so the teachers don't see her. Suddenly she sees Henry pushing his wheelbarrow and Miss Sharp is with him. Fiona recognizes her **hooded** raincoat. They walk to the middle of the field. Miss Sharp gives Henry a **car jack** and he uses it to move a heavy stone. Then he and Miss Sharp lift something out of the wheelbarrow... a body! They throw it into the well." She laughs. "**Ridiculous**! My sweet brother and the headmistress throwing a body into the well! I told Fiona she was **mad**. 'You dreamt it!' I said."

Hudson picks up his phone. "Baker, go to the Sunshine Retirement Home in Shepton Mallet. Please get Miss Sharp and bring her in for questioning."

Hudson turns back to Mrs Motherwell. "Why did Fiona come to you? Why didn't she go straight to the police?"

"Fiona was only 11. She wanted to talk to someone she **trusted**."

"And she trusted you?" asks Hudson.

"Yes, I was the only person at the school that she trusted – me and her friend Claire. So she came to tell me first."

"And you told her she was a wicked girl and a murderer, right?"

"Right!" Mrs Motherwell replies with a nasty smile.

"So you bullied Fiona to stop her telling the police about Henry?" Hudson asks. "And you were protecting Miss Sharp, too?"

"Heather Sharp is my friend," she replies loudly. "She was the only one who gave Henry a chance."

"Tell me about Miss Foster. Did Henry and Miss Sharp kill her?"

"Of course not! How ridiculous! Henry wouldn't hurt a fly. And Heather was a very strict headmistress but not a killer."

"So who killed the teacher then?" Matthews asks.

Mrs Motherwell does not answer.

"Emily Foster was Rebecca's class teacher, wasn't she?" Hudson asks.

Mrs Motherwell sits in silence and doesn't react.

Exercise 47: Correct the mistakes. Lesen Sie weiter und korrigieren Sie die sechs Fehler!

"This is what I thing," says Hudson, watching Mrs Motherwell careful. "Miss Foster new something about who Rebecca died. Perhaps it wasn't a accident. Perhaps Henry killed the girl and her teacher found out. That's why Miss Foster had to died. Right?"

1. _____   4. _____

2. _____   5. _____

3. _____   6. _____

"**How dare you!**" Mrs Motherwell shouts. "You're just like she was. Stupid young woman... saying such bad things about Henry!"

"What did Miss Foster say about Henry?" Hudson asks quietly.

"She comes to the office one evening and says she wants to talk to Miss Sharp, but Heather is out. She seems upset so I ask her to sit down and tell me what's wrong. 'It's Henry. I saw him on the night of the accident,' she says. 'I think he hurt Becky. I'm going to tell the police.' 'Please don't do that!' I **beg**. But she

to beg	(an)flehen
briefcase	Aktentasche
Board of Directors	Aufsichtsrat
trial period	Probezeit
to confess	gestehen

won't listen to me. 'I'm not waiting any longer,' she says... and she leaves."

"But Miss Foster never went to the police, did she?" Hudson asks. "You stopped her, didn't you? You killed her and hid her body. Then you wrote a letter to say that she had gone to Australia."

"That's a lie! I never did any of that!" she shouts, hysterical now.

Hudson opens his **briefcase** and takes out two pieces of paper. He puts them on the table in front of her.

"This is Miss Foster's resignation letter," he says pointing at an old piece of writing paper. "And this is the note that Penny left at the hotel last week to say that she had to go back to work. Matthews, what do you think about that?"

"It's the same handwriting," Matthews answers.

"Exactly. And this...," Hudson takes a third piece of paper out of his pocket, "...is a shopping list I found lying on your desk this afternoon, Mrs Motherwell. It's the same handwriting, too. You wrote all of these notes, didn't you?"

For a moment there is silence in the interview room. Hudson and Matthews hold their breath, waiting. Then at last she starts to talk.

"It's a warm June evening in 1985. Heather invites Henry and me to her office for a glass of sherry. We're celebrating Henry's new job as school caretaker. She says the **Board of Directors** are happy to give him a six-month **trial period**. All he has to do is work hard and stay out of trouble. We drink to that. Then Henry and I stand up to leave. I open the office door and that little girl is standing there. She's sleepwalking again. She wakes up suddenly. She's frightened and she doesn't know where she is. When she sees a tall man standing in front of her, she opens her mouth to scream. 'Calm down girl, it's only Henry!' I say and I step towards her. But she steps backwards. And then she's falling... Heather runs out of the office and sees Rebecca lying at the bottom of the stairs. 'Go home at once!' she says to Henry and he runs off to the cottage."

"So Rebecca's death really was an accident, then?" Hudson asks.

"Of course it was. But Heather knew that people would suspect Henry if he was at the scene. That's why she sent him home. But it didn't help. There are so many stupid people in the world."

"Like Emily Foster, you mean?" Hudson asks.

Mrs Motherwell nods.

"So either you killed her or Henry did," Hudson continues. "Which of you is the killer? Tell me the truth, Mrs Motherwell."

She puts her head in her hands. "Emily made me really angry, you know. 'Why do so many people think badly of my brother? He's a sweet and gentle man,' I say. But she won't listen to me. She tries to leave. What could I do? I try to hold her back but she hits me hard. Then she breaks away and tries to run out of the room. It all happens so fast. I don't have any time to think. I just know that I have to stop her. So I pick up a tennis trophy from the shelf next to me and I hit her on the back of her head. She falls down dead."

"Well done, Hudson. She's confessed to everything," Matthews says half an hour later in the corridor. He and Hudson watch as two officers lead Mrs Motherwell away.

"Thanks, but I'm afraid that's not the end of my day's work."

They walk towards the reception desk where someone is complaining in a loud, angry voice.

"Why am I here, young man? Explain at once!"

"Ah, Miss Sharp, thank you for coming," Hudson says politely. "I'd like to talk to you about your friend Mrs Motherwell."

"Good luck, Inspector," says Matthews as Hudson takes Miss Sharp into an interview room.

Exercise 48: True or false? Welche Aussagen sind korrekt? Markieren Sie mit richtig ✔ oder falsch – !

1. Miss Foster told Miss Sharp about Henry. ❏

2. Mrs Motherwell didn't like Miss Sharp. ❏

3. Henry killed Rebecca Bracknell. ❏

4. Miss Sharp tried to protect Henry. ❏

"Thank you for your help, doctor," Hudson says to Willerby two hours later outside Fiona's room at the hospital. "She wouldn't talk to me until you came. But now we know the whole story."

"She has a phobia about people in authority, like teachers or policemen," the doctor explains. "That's probably why she sent you those messages about the well. She couldn't tell you directly."

"Did you know about the body in the well? Did Fiona tell you about it during her therapy?" Hudson asks.

"Yes, she did. But I never believed her. I thought she made the story up because she hated that school so much. I never believed she was telling the truth." He looks ashamed.

"Excuse me, Dr Willerby. I have to make a call," Hudson says. He walks a few steps away and dials Matthews' number.

"Hudson here, I've just finished talking to Mrs Lambert."

"How is she?" Matthews asks.

"Just a few cuts and bruises, nothing serious. And she has told me everything. For 30 years she tried hard to forget about 1985. She really believed what Mrs Motherwell told her – that she was responsible for Becky's death. But when she saw Penny at the open day, all the **memories** came back. And when Claire told her that Penny was a successful lawyer, Fiona thought, 'Perhaps Penny can help me to **uncover** the past'. But she knew that Penny hated

people in authority	Autoritäts-personen
to make sth. up	eine Geschichte erfinden
to look ashamed	beschämt aussehen
memories *pl*	Erinnerungen
to uncover	aufdecken

her when they were young, so she couldn't talk to her directly. Instead Fiona sent her a message. And then another one. And after that she felt braver and asked Penny to meet her at the pub."

"So they met at the Queen's Arms?"

"That's right," Hudson says. "Fiona was scared that Penny wouldn't believe her. But Penny was very interested in the story. She asked Fiona to show her where it had happened, so they left the pub. And because it was raining they took Penny's car. At the field near the well, they sat in the car while Fiona described what she had seen."

"How did Penny react to that?" Matthews asks.

"She wanted to go to the school straight away and tell Miss Musty. That's when Fiona lost her nerve. She said, 'No! I don't want anything to do with that school again.' So Penny decided to go there alone and Fiona went home on foot. That was the last time she saw her. Fiona had no idea what had happened to Penny."

"Good morning, everybody," says Hudson on Monday at Scotland Yard. "Team, I'd like you to meet Inspector Matthews, Constable Baker and Constable Stewart. They have been working with me in Shepton Mallet."

debriefing session	Abschlussbesprechung
to confirm	bestätigen
to feel sorry for sb.	mit jdm. Mitleid haben

The policemen from Somerset and London shake hands.

"Now, let's get started with the **debriefing session**," says Hudson.

"I've got a question, sir," says DI Jarvis. "Was Rebecca Bracknell's death an accident, like Mrs Motherwell said?"

"Yes, Miss Sharp **confirmed** Mrs Motherwell's story."

"What did Mrs Motherwell do after she killed Miss Foster?" asks Bradley.

"Well, she had to get rid of the body somehow. So she told Henry to fetch his wheelbarrow and together they took it to the well."

"But why did Fiona think it was Miss Sharp who threw the body in the well?" asks DI Jarvis.

"That evening it was raining," Hudson explains. "So Mrs Motherwell put on her friend's raincoat which was hanging in the office. And that's what Fiona saw – someone wearing Miss Sharp's raincoat."

"Didn't Mrs Motherwell tell Miss Sharp what had happened?"

"No, she didn't," Hudson replies. "All these years Miss Sharp really believed that Emily Foster had gone to Australia."

"And what about Penny Sutton?" Jarvis asks. "She went to the school to talk to Miss Musty about Fiona's story, didn't she?"

"Yes, but that night she met Mrs Motherwell before she had a chance to speak to Miss Musty," Inspector Matthews explains.

"Yes," says Hudson. "For 30 years Mrs Motherwell hid Miss Foster's death. So when Penny Sutton turned up [i] at the school asking questions, she had to kill her, too."

"So she hit Penny on the head and put her body in the boot of her own car?" Bradley asks.

"Yes, exactly," Hudson says. "Then she parked Penny's car next to the field, and Henry took Penny to the well in his wheelbarrow."

"But why did Mrs Motherwell kidnap Fiona?" asks Jarvis.

"When I arrived in the village looking for Penny, Fiona wanted to contact me," Hudson explains. "Remember how she led me to the well? Mrs Motherwell found out about it and wanted to stop her."

Exercise 49: Which term is correct? Welcher der Begriffe ist korrekt? Unterstreichen Sie!

1. car shoe   car boot   car space
2. handcuffs   handgloves   hand shells
3. key bundle   key band   key ring
4. hockey stock   hockey stick   hockey bat

"Now I've got some questions for you," Hudson says. "Jarvis, what's the news about Mr Wiley. Is he still missing?"

"No, sir, we found him yesterday back at his allotment. He's very sorry for everything and wants to make a new start with his wife."

"Oh dear, I hope Brenda Wiley doesn't say yes," Hudson says. "Don't worry, sir. Mrs Wiley has a new lawyer now. It's Penny's boss, Mr Corbett. The court case is next Thursday."

"Good luck to her," says Hudson. "And what about Mr Sutton? I feel quite sorry for him."

Phrasal Verbs
Das Verb **to turn** wird mit verschiedenen Präpositionen verwendet:

to turn up	auftauchen
to turn off	ausschalten
to turn over	umdrehen
to turn into	sich verwandeln in
to turn down	ablehnen

"Yes," says Jarvis. "Poor Sutton... his wife's death and then the murder investigation. He's staying with his sister in Manchester until after the funeral."

funeral	Beerdigung
prison	Gefängnis
cheeky	frech

"I've got a question, too," says Inspector Matthews. "Mrs Motherwell left Penny Sutton's car at the scrapyard, didn't she?"

"Yes, that's right," answers Bradley. "And Henry was the man I saw on film sitting next to her on the passenger seat."

"But how did they get home from Basingstoke without a car?"

"The train station is just a mile from the scrapyard," Bradley explains. "So they walked there and waited for the first morning train back to Warminster."

"Any more questions?" Hudson asks.

"Just one," says WPC Harvey. "What will happen to Henry if his sister goes to prison?"

"I was worried about that, too," Hudson admits. "But Miss Musty says she will take care of Henry. And you know what? I think he may even be happier without Mrs Motherwell."

Ein **pink elephant** meint entweder etwas ganz außergewöhnliches oder bezeichnet Halluzinationen, die man unter Drogeneinfluss hat.

He looks around the room at his colleagues. "That was a difficult case, but together we solved it. You all did some very good work. So I'm taking you all out for a nice pub lunch at the Pink Elephant!"[1]

"But sir, you never drink on duty!" says Harvey with a cheeky grin.

"There's always a first time," Hudson replies with a laugh.

Final Test

Exercise 1: Who did what? Verbinden Sie Täter und Aktion!

1. ☐ crashed the car   **a)** no one

2. ☐ made aggressive phone calls   **b)** the chambermaid

3. ☐ found Penny's phone   **c)** some teenagers

4. ☐ killed Rebecca Bracknell   **d)** Mr Wiley

Exercise 2: Translation. Übersetzen Sie!

1. Margaret gab ihnen ihre Visitenkarte.

2. Die Schülerinnen hatten Angst vor der Schulleiterin.

3. Was zum Teufel macht er hinter dem Zaun?

4. Miss Musty und Miss Foster waren eng befreundet.

5. Sie sind damit beschäftigt, den Schubkarren zu untersuchen.

Exercise 3: Boarding School. Finden Sie neun Begriffe zum Thema Internat!

B	A	F	E	H	E	T	C	O	S	E	L	Y	L
O	S	T	U	E	M	U	L	E	P	R	E	T	O
T	C	I	D	A	O	N	A	L	O	T	S	S	Y
S	H	E	A	D	M	I	S	T	R	E	S	S	X
Y	O	R	M	G	P	F	S	A	T	A	O	R	O
D	O	R	M	I	T	O	R	Y	S	C	N	E	Y
O	L	M	E	R	T	R	O	U	S	H	B	A	Q
R	T	A	A	L	E	M	O	M	A	E	R	Y	A
L	E	D	A	R	E	T	M	E	N	R	P	E	S

Exercise 4: Multiple choice. Welcher Satz ist korrekt? Kreuzen Sie an!

1. a) ☐ Miss Paddington is interesting in Hudson's work.
   b) ☐ Miss Paddington is interested in Hudson's work.

2. a) ☐ Penny turned up at the school.
   b) ☐ Penny turned off at the school.

3. a) ☐ The police is looking for the murder.
   b) ☐ The police are looking for the murderer.

4. a) ☐ Penny is dead, I'm afraid.
   b) ☐ Penny is dead, I'm frightened.

Exercise 5: Where is Shepton Mallet? Lösen Sie das Kreuzworträtsel!

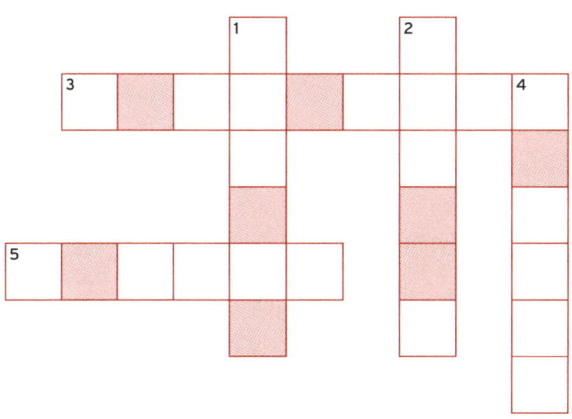

Lösung: ___ ___ ___ ___ ___ ___ ___ ___

Across:

3. DI Bradley would like to have an ...

5. If you do something illegal, you ... a crime.

Down:

1. Penny was the ... of a violent crime.

2. Miss Musty was only interested in her ...

4. Mrs Motherwell killed Miss Foster with the sports ...

Exercise 6: Definitions. Schreiben Sie das beschriebene Wort auf!

1. This helps you to see something far away. _____

2. A step up in your career. _____

3. A very small town. _____

4. The political leader of the UK. _____

 **Answers**

Exercise 1:	lovely, blue, young, ugly, grey, yellow, terrible, bossy, arrogant
Exercise 2:	1. at 2. through 3. on 4. behind 5. above
Exercise 3:	1. true 2. false (Miss Foster was very popular.) 3. true 4. false (Penny is a lawyer.)
Exercise 4:	1. get 2. leads 3. is standing 4. pours
Exercise 5:	1. them 2. it 3. her 4. They
Exercise 6:	1. morning 2. watch 3. thinks 4. Perhaps 5. reception
Exercise 7:	1. She is the headmistress of Shepton Mallet Boarding School for Girls.
	2. She meets Fiona at the Queen's Arms pub.
	3. Fiona thinks Penny was a teacher's pet.
	4. She finds it in room 14 when she is cleaning.
Exercise 8:	1. is 2. knocks 3. were 4. found 5. thought
Exercise 9:	1. c 2. d 3. a 4. b
Exercise 10:	1. is standing (standing) 2. give (gives) 3. 14-year-old boy (14-years-old boy) 4. a lot of (lot of) 5. through (threw) 6. mobile (handy)
Exercise 11:	1. emergency 2. pile 3. proud 4. message **Lösung:** clue
Exercise 12:	1. b 2. a 3. d 4. c
Exercise 13:	1. I've 2. he's 3. You're 4. It's 5. you'll
Exercise 14:	1. colleague 2. husband 3. assistant 4. boss
Exercise 15:	1. Was ist los? 2. Sie macht ihre Sache gut. 3. Macht nichts! 4. Ich komme einfach nicht voran!
Exercise 16:	1. turns off 2. walks 3. replies 4. is 5. go
Exercise 17:	1. d 2. c 3. b 4. a

Exercise 18: 1. what 2. Why 3. What 4. Who 5. What
Exercise 19: 1. rings 2. calling 3. loved 4. than
Exercise 20: 1. surprise 2. number 3. text 4. message
Exercise 21:

1 N	2 E	3 T	4 B	5 A	6 L
20 Y	21 E	22 L	23 L	24 O	7 L
19 C	32 B	33 E	34 C	25 W	8 I
18 N	31 E	36 A	35 C	26 O	9 T
17 E	30 R	29 E	28 D	27 N	10 T
16 G	15 R	14 E	13 M	12 E	11 L

Exercise 22: 1. hard 2. heavy 3. terrible 4. closer 5. deep 6. dark
Exercise 23: 1. bottom 2. late 3. serious 4. dangerous 5. death
6. find
Exercise 24: 1. d 2. b 3. a 4. c
Exercise 25: 1. Next Hudson drives back to Scotland Yard.
2. He meets Jarvis outside an interview room.
3. "Morning, sir!" she says brightly.
4. "Morning, Jarvis. How is Mr Wiley this morning?"
Exercise 26: 1. d 2. c 3. a 4. b
Exercise 27: 1. seat 2. office 3. shakes 4. breath 5. crime
Exercise 28: 1. I spent the weekend sitting at my computer.
2. She tries to escape.
3. He keeps complaining.
4. I am renting a small flat.
Exercise 29: 1. b 2. d 3. a 4. c
Exercise 30: 1. new (knew) 2. to (too) 3. of (off) 4. right (write)
5. her (she) 6. know (no)
Exercise 31: 1. true 2. false. (He has no idea who she was.)
3. false. (She doesn't find one.) 4. true
Exercise 32: 1. arrives 2. thick 3. round 4. hard 5. sits down
Exercise 33: 1. arrival 2. choice 3. thought 4. reply 5. death
6. connection
Exercise 34: 1. window 2. receptionist 3. windowsill 4. afternoon
Exercise 35: 1. scared 2. important 3. unusual 4. continue

Exercise 36: 1. quiet 2. here 3. some 4. me 5. sadly

Exercise 37: 1. d 2. a 3. b 4. c

Exercise 38: 1. edge 2. behind 3. get out 4. busy 5. want to wait

Exercise 39: 1. firm 2. nervous 3. strong 4. tight

Exercise 40: 1. leaving 2. rings 3. is 4. have 5. missing 6. thought

Exercise 41: 1. b 2. d 3. a 4. c

Exercise 42: 1. tray 2. truth 3. persuade 4. accident
5. reputation 6. harmless 7. liar
Lösung: Australia

Exercise 43: 1. told 2. argument 3. about 4. died 5. upset

Exercise 44: 1. Übrigens, ich heiße Nancy.
2. Reiß dich zusammen!
3. Jetzt kommen wir endlich voran.
4. Ich hole die Schlüssel.

Exercise 45: 1. past 2. towards 3. Next to 4. in 5. in 6. at

Exercise 46: 1. hysterically 2. stupid 3. gentle 4. broken
5. tightly

Exercise 47: 1. think (thing) 2. carefully (careful) 3. knew (new)
4. how (who) 5. an (a) 6. die (died)

Exercise 48: 1. false (Mrs Motherwell killed her before she could
talk to Miss Sharp.) 2. false (They were friends.)
3. false (It was an accident.) 4. true

Exercise 49: 1. car boot 2. handcuffs 3. key ring
4. hockey stick

Final Test

Exercise 1:   **1.** c **2.** d **3.** b **4.** a

Exercise 2:   **1.** Margaret gave them her business card. **2.** The schoolgirls were afraid of the headmistress.
3. What on earth is he doing behind the fence?
4. Miss Musty and Miss Foster were close friends.
5. They are busy examining the wheelbarrow.

Exercise 3:

B	A	F	E	H	E	T	C	O	S	E	L	Y
O	S	T	U	E	M	U	L	E	P	R	E	T
T	C	I	D	A	O	N	A	L	O	T	S	S
S	H	E	A	D	M	I	S	T	R	E	S	S
Y	O	R	M	G	P	F	S	A	T	A	O	R
D	O	R	M	I	T	O	R	Y	S	C	N	E
O	L	M	E	R	T	R	O	U	S	H	B	A
R	T	A	A	L	E	M	O	M	A	E	R	Y
L	E	D	A	R	E	T	M	E	N	R	P	E

Exercise 4:   **1.** b **2.** a **3.** b **4.** a

Exercise 5:

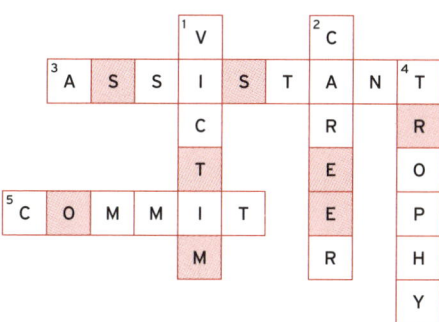

Lösung: Somerset

Exercise 6:   **1.** binoculars **2.** promotion **3.** village
4. prime minister

Glossary

⚡ = umgangssprachlich

pl = Plural

accelerator	Gaspedal
allotment	Schrebergarten
anxious	besorgt, ängstlich
APB (all points bulletin)	Fahndungsaufruf
appointment	Termin
armed	bewaffnet
to arrest	festnehmen
asap	schnellstmöglich
assembly hall	Aula
attached	befestigt
awful	furchtbar
bald	kahlköpfig
to be blindfolded	die Augen verbunden haben
to be deep in conversation	ins Gespräch vertieft sein
to beg	(an)flehen
to be in a terrible hurry	es schrecklich eilig haben
to be in charge	die Verantwortung tragen
to be just about to	gerade dabei sein, etw. zu tun
to bet (bet, bet)	wetten
binoculars *pl*	Fernglas
bloodstain	Blutfleck
blow	Schlag
Board of Directors	Aufsichtsrat
boarding school	Internat
body	*hier*: Leichnam

bossy	bestimmend, herrisch
bottom	Boden
bow tie	Fliege
breathlessly	atemlos
briefcase	Aktentasche
bruise	blauer Fleck
to bully	mobben, schikanieren
to bump into	zusammenstoßen mit
to bury	begraben
business card	Visitenkarte
by force	mit Gewalt
to cancel	absagen
car boot	Kofferraum
caretaker	Hausmeister
car jack	Wagenheber
to carve	meißeln
case	Fall
to catch one's foot	mit dem Fuß hängenbleiben
cause of death	Todesursache
CCTV (closed-circuit television)	Überwachungskamera
chambermaid	Zimmermädchen
to change the subject	das Thema wechseln
to chat	sich unterhalten, plaudern
cheek	Wange
cheeky	frech
choir	Chor
churchyard	Friedhof
closely	genau
clue	Hinweis
coincidence	Zufall
to collapse	zusammenbrechen
to come to no good	böse enden
to commit a crime	ein Verbrechen begehen
to compare	vergleichen
to complain	sich beschweren
comprehensive school	Gesamtschule
concrete paving slab	Betonplatte
to confess	gestehen

confidential	vertraulich
to confirm	bestätigen
connection	Verbindung
Constabulary	Polizeirevier
to cordon off	absperren
cottage	Häuschen, kleines Landhaus
council	Gemeinderat
court	*hier*: Gericht
cover	Abdeckung
to creep up to	sich anschleichen an
crime scene	Tatort
crime	Verbrechen
cruel	grausam
CU (see you)	wir sehen uns
curious	neugierig
curly	lockig
database	Datenbank
debriefing session	Abschlussbesprechung
denim jacket	Jeansjacke
deputy	Stellvertreter(in)
desperately	verzweifelt
to dial	wählen
to dig	graben
to disappear	verschwinden
to disturb	stören
diving squad	Polizeitaucher
divorce	Scheidung
dormitory	Schlafsaal
doubt	Zweifel
to drop	fallen lassen
to drown	ertrinken
to earn	verdienen
edge	Rand, Kante
to educate	(aus)bilden
elderly	ältere(r,s)
emergency	Notfall
enemy	Feind
envelope	Umschlag

equipment	Ausrüstung
to escape	fliehen, flüchten
evidence	Beweis
to examine	untersuchen
excited	aufgeregt, begeistert
to exclaim	ausrufen (Schock od. Überraschung)
to expect	erwarten
factory	Fabrik
to feel sorry for sb.	mit jdm. Mitleid haben
fence	Zaun
to fetch	herbeiholen
filing cabinet	Aktenschrank
firmly	fest
fist	Faust
forehead	Stirn
Foreign Office *UK*	Außenministerium
forensic	gerichtsmedizinisch
former	ehemalig
frame by frame	Bild für Bild
to frown	die Stirn runzeln
funeral	Beerdigung
gagged	geknebelt
to gasp	nach Luft schnappen, kurz einatmen
gate	Tor
gently	sanft
to get drunk	sich betrinken
to get in touch	Kontakt aufnehmen
to get one's hands on sb.	jmd. in die Finger kriegen
to get on with sb.	mit jmd. auskommen
to get rid of	loswerden
⚡ to get somewhere	vorankommen (mit etw.)
ghostly	unheimlich
⚡ good-for-nothing	Taugenichts
gossip	Klatsch
grades *pl*	*hier*: Noten
gravestone	Grabstein
grimly	grimmig
habit	Gewohnheit

halfway human	halbwegs menschlich
handicapped	behindert
handicrafts *pl*	Handarbeiten
to handcuff sb.	jmd. Handschellen anlegen
handle	Griff
headache	Kopfweh
head girl	Schulsprecherin
headmistress	Schulleiterin
height	Größe, Höhe
He wouldn't hurt a fly.	Er kann keiner Fliege etwas zuleide tun.
to hold on tight	fest halten
hooded	mit Kapuze
hosepipe	Wasserschlauch
housekeeper	Haushälterin
How dare you!	Was erlauben Sie sich!
to hurt (hurt, hurt)	wehtun
identity parade	polizeiliche Gegenüberstellung
to imagine	sich vorstellen
impatiently	ungeduldig
in person	persönlich
in silence	schweigend
to insist	auf etw. bestehen
in tears	in Tränen aufgelöst
instead	stattdessen
intercom	Gegensprechanlage
investigation	Ermittlung
it's not like her	es ist nicht ihre Art
jealous	neidisch
to join in	mitmachen
to joyride	eine Spritztour machen
key ring	Schlüsselbund
to kick sb. out	jmd. rausschmeißen
lab	Labor
landlord	*hier*: Wirt
law firm	Anwaltskanzlei
lawn	Rasen
lawyer	Anwalt/Anwältin

lazy	faul
leather	Leder
Let's take her for a spin.	Lass uns eine Spritztour machen.
letter of resignation	Kündigungsbrief
liar	Lügner(in)
link	Verbindung
to lock up	abschließen
loner	Einzelgänger(in)
to look ashamed	beschämt aussehen
to look blank	verständnislos schauen
mad	verrückt
to magnify	vergrößern
magpie	Elster
maiden name	Geburtsname
to make fun of sb.	sich über jmd. lustig machen
to make sth. up	eine Geschichte erfinden
manners *pl*	Benehmen
marble	Marmor
⚡ mate	Kumpel
meanwhile	währenddessen
memories *pl*	Erinnerungen
mess	Unordnung
middle-aged	mittleren Alters
to mind one's own business	sich um seine eigenen Angele-genheiten kümmern
miserable	elend
mood	Laune
moustache	Oberlippenbart
to move out	ausziehen
to mow the lawn	Rasen mähen
My goodness!	Meine Güte!
nasty	böse
neat and tidy	ordentlich, picobello
necessary	notwendig
neither ... nor	weder ... noch
Never mind.	Macht nichts.
next-of-kin	nächster Angehörige
nightmare	Albtraum

night-watchman	Nachtwächter
noisy	laut
to notice	(be)merken
oak	Eiche
on duty	im Dienst
only child	Einzelkind
open day	Tag der offenen Tür
ordinary	normal, gewöhnlich
out of breath	atemlos
outgoing calls *pl*	ausgehende Anrufe
to oversleep (-slept, -slept)	verschlafen
to overtake (-took, -taken)	überholen
pale	blass
PC (police constable)	Polizeibeamte(r)
peeping Tom	Spanner
people in authority	Autoritätspersonen
to persuade sb.	jmd. überreden
⚡ Phew!	Uff!
physically	körperlich
⚡ pig	*hier*: Bulle
pile	Haufen
polite	höflich
prime minister	Premierminister(in)
prime suspect	Hauptverdächtige(r)
prison	Gefängnis
probably	wahrscheinlich
progress	Fortschritt
to promise	versprechen
promotion	Beförderung
to protect	schützen
protective clothing	Schutzbekleidung
proudly	stolz
to pull oneself together	sich zusammenreißen
⚡ to put sb. behind bars	jmd. hinter Gitter bringen
puzzled	verblüfft, verwirrt
Rather you than me!	Lieber Sie als ich!
to reach for sth.	nach etw. greifen
recent	aktuell

recently	in letzter Zeit
to recognize	wiedererkennen
record	*hier*: Akte
registration number	Autokennzeichen
relationship	Beziehung
relative	Verwandte(r)
relieved	erleichtert
reluctantly	widerwillig
to rent	mieten
reputation	Ruf
resident	Bewohner(in)
responsible	verantwortlich
to retire	in Rente gehen
Retirement Home	Altersheim
to rewind (rewound, rewound)	zurückspulen
ridiculous	lächerlich
rocking chair	Schaukelstuhl
row	Reihe
rude	unhöflich
sample	Probe
to scare sb. to death	jmd. zu Tode erschrecken
school fees *pl*	Schulgebühren
scrapyard	Schrottplatz
scratch	Kratzer
to scratch	kratzen
search warrant	Durchsuchungsbefehl
security guard	Sicherheitsbedienstete(r)
separated	getrennt
to set (set, set) a date	einen Termin festlegen
shaky	zitternd
shape	Form
shed	Schuppen
shelf	Regal
shepherd's pie	Auflauf mit Lammfleisch und Kartoffelbrei
shoulder-length	schulterlang
to shudder	schaudern
shy	schüchtern

to sigh	seufzen
sight	Anblick
sign	Zeichen, Hinweis
to sign	unterschreiben
silk	Seide
to sip	nippen
skull	Schädel
to sleepwalk	schlafwandeln
sleeve	Ärmel
smart	*hier*: schick
sober	nüchtern
to solve	lösen
⚡ So what?!	Ja und?!
to speed (sped, sped)	rasen
to spit (spat, spat)	spuken
splinter	Splitter
squad car	Streifenwagen
staff	Personal
stall	Verkaufsstand
startled	erschrocken
state	Zustand
to stay in touch	in Kontakt bleiben
stern	streng
straight away	sofort
strange	merkwürdig, seltsam
strict	streng
to stub out	ausdrücken
success	Erfolg
successful	erfolgreich
surrounded by	umgeben von
suspicious	verdächtig
suspicious of	misstrauisch gegenüber
to swallow	schlucken
sweat	Schweiß
swollen	angeschwollen
tap	Wasserhahn
to tap	klopfen, tippen
⚡ teacher's pet	Lehrers Liebling, Streberin

That's a shame!	Wie schade!
The time is up.	Die Zeit ist abgelaufen.
thoughtfully	nachdenklich
to threaten	drohen
throat	Hals
tiled	gefliest
tongue	Zunge
torch	Taschenlampe
to trace	aufspüren
track	Spur
tray	Tablett
trial period	Probezeit
trial	Gerichtsverfahren
to trust	vertrauen
truth	Wahrheit
to uncover	aufdecken
underage	minderjährig
to unlock	aufschließen
upset	aufgebracht
urgently	dringend
versus	gegen
victim	Opfer
villager	Dorfbewohner(in)
violent crime	Gewaltverbrechen
wallet	Portemonnaie
wedding	Hochzeit
weeds	Unkraut
well	Brunnen
What on earth...!	Was zum Teufel...?!
⚡ What's up?	Was ist los?
wheelbarrow	Schubkarre
to whisper	flüstern
wicked	böse
windowsill	Fensterbank
witness	Zeuge
to wonder	sich fragen
wood	kleiner Wald
wooden	aus Holz
wrinkled	runzelig

List of Exercises

Final Test

Lernkrimi Lektüren Englisch

A1

Death at Land's End
Kurzkrimis
ISBN 978-3-8174-9658-7

The Murderer Next Door
Kurzkrimis
ISBN 978-3-8174-9438-5

A2

Blood and Breakfast
Kurzkrimis
ISBN 978-3-8174-7760-9

Murder at Teatime
Kurzkrimis
ISBN 978-3-8174-7839-2

Deadly Business
Kurzkrimis
ISBN 978-3-8174-9215-2

Long Time No Kill
Classic
ISBN 978-3-8174-9794-2

It Was Murder, My Lord
Kurzkrimis
ISBN 978-3-8174-7734-0

Murderous Collection
Sammelband 10 in 1
ISBN 978-3-8174-8967-1

Last Exit Waterloo Bridge
Kurzkrimis
ISBN 978-3-8174-7733-3

Bullets over Bristol
Kurzkrimis
ISBN 978-3-8174-8544-4

Death Comes Knocking
Kurzkrimis
ISBN 978-3-8174-7945-0

Murderous Network
Kurzkrimis
ISBN 978-3-8174-9312-8

Der Rächer von Canterbury
Classic
ISBN 978-3-8174-7662-6

B1

Art and Ashes
Classic
ISBN 978-3-8174-9493-4

Der rote Nebel
Classic
ISBN 978-3-8174-7574-2

Cook and Kill
Classic
ISBN 978-3-8174-9492-7

Ein fast perfekter Coup
Classic
ISBN 978-3-8174-7568-1

Crime Scene Tower of London
Classic
ISBN 978-3-8174-7687-9

Game Over in Soho
Classic
ISBN 978-3-8174-7878-1

Deadly Mistake
Classic
ISBN 978-3-8174-8259-7

Hunting the Vampire
Classic
ISBN 978-3-8174-7305-2

Death Wasn't the Deal
Classic
ISBN 978-3-8174-9491-0

The Mystery of the Mummy
Classic
ISBN 978-3-8174-7304-5

Lernkrimi Lektüren Englisch

Lernkrimi Hörbücher Englisch

A2

A Shot in the Night
ISBN 978-3-8174-8202-3

Death Wish
ISBN 978-3-8174-8204-7

The Butterworth Mystery
ISBN 978-3-8174-8203-0

Strangled
ISBN 978-3-8174-9665-5

B1

Bloody Revenge
ISBN 978-3-8174-8860-5

Danger at King's Cross
ISBN 978-3-8174-7673-2

The Thames Murderer
ISBN 978-3-8174-7674-9

B2

Bloody Legacy
ISBN 978-3-8174-7676-3

Crime & Company
ISBN 978-3-8174-8976-3

Die Intrigantin
ISBN 978-3-8174-7675-6

Murder at the Office
ISBN 978-3-8174-7747-0

Lernkrimi Rätselblöcke Englisch

A1

Murderous Games
ISBN 978-3-8174-9500-9

A2

The Art of Crime
ISBN 978-3-8174-9155-1

B1

A Deadly Puzzle
ISBN 978-3-8174-8832-2

Lernkrimi Sprachkurs Englisch

A1/A2

Lernkrimi Sprachkurs
ISBN 978-3-8174-7844-5